Great Michigan Deer Tales

Book 3

Great Michigan Deer Tales Book 3

Stories Behind Michigan's Biggest Bucks

Richard P. Smith

Smith Publications

Great Michigan Deer Tales - Book 3
Stories Behind Michigan's Biggest Bucks

by Richard P. Smith

Published by:
Smith Publications
Richard P. Smith
Lucy J. La Faive
814 Clark St.
Marquette, MI 49855

All rights reserved. No part of this book may be reproduced or transmitted in any form or any means, electronic or mechanical, including photocopying, recording or by any information storage and retrieval system without written permission from the author, except for the inclusion of brief quotations in a review.

Copyright © 2001 by Richard P. Smith
First Printing 2001
Printed in the United States of America

All photos by the author unless otherwise credited
Cover photo by Richard P. Smith
Back cover design plan by Lucy J. La Faive
Book production & design by Lucy J. La Faive
Interior Layout by Globe Printing, Inc.

Printed on recycled paper

Library of Congress Cataloging in Publication Data
Smith, Richard P.
Great Michigan Deer Tales - Book 3 : Stories Behind Michigan's Biggest Bucks / by Richard P. Smith
Deer hunting—Michigan
SK 301.S6 2001 bk.3   799.27SM bk.3
ISBN 0-9710355-0-4 Softcover

FOR TIRA O'BRIEN,
*the person who enters trophy
bucks in state records
and is the voice of CBM!*

Contents

Chapter 1 - THE ROMPOLA BUCK	10
Chapter 2 - ROMPOLA CONTINUED	20
Chapter 3 - BRANCH COUNTY MUZZLELOADER RECORDS	34
Chapter 4 - FATHER/SON TROPHY	44
Chapter 5 - A HAPPY 14-YEAR-OLD	50
Chapter 6 - THUMBS UP BOONERS	56
Chapter 7 - THE BOLLINGER BUCK	64
Chapter 8 - MICHIGAN'S HANSON BUCK	70
Chapter 9 - MONROE COUNTY MONSTER	76
Chapter 10 - BIGGEST NONTYPICALS FROM 1997	80
Chapter 11 - BEGINNER'S LUCK BOONER	88
Chapter 12 - A BUCK NAMED LUCKY	96
Chapter 13 - OAKLAND COUNTY BOONER	102
Chapter 14 - EXPERT SENIOR CITIZEN	108
Chapter 15 - BARAGA COUNTY NONTYPICALS	116
About The Author	124
Books By The Author	126

Acknowledgments

First and foremost I would like to acknowledge and thank all officers and measurers, past and present, of Commemorative Bucks of Michigan (CBM) for their efforts in measuring many of the big antlered bucks bagged in the state each year and for maintaining a dependable set of records that are becoming an increasingly valuable reference for all big game hunters interested in trying their luck in Michigan. These records help promote the state and give it the credit that's due as a quality whitetail producer. Through the help of CBM, especially Records Coordinator Tira O'Brien, I have been able to locate and interview some of the hunters mentioned in this book.

CBM's records are referred to frequently on the pages that follow to help put the size of the racks that are discussed in perspective. How the antlers rank in the county where they were taken and on a statewide basis is mentioned in most, if not all, cases. However, those rankings can change from year-to-year and those that appear in the chapters of this book were current at the time the book was written.

Hunters do not have to have bagged a buck or any other trophy animal that qualifies for state records to belong to CBM. Annual memberships are $20. To join, send a check or money order to CBM, P.O. Box 518, Dryden, MI 48428. For additional information call 810-796-2925 or 800-298-2925.

If you have bagged a buck with antlers that might qualify for listing in state records, you should have the rack measured. It doesn't matter what year the deer was killed.

A list of CBM's statewide network of scorers, along with their addresses and telephone numbers, should be available at most DNR offices. Contact the CBM representative nearest you to make an appointment to have your antlers measured. All racks taken during the current season must air dry for 60 days before they can be officially scored. The deadline for each year's scoring period is March 31. There's a $5 charge to enter antlers in state records that meet minimum qualifications for hunters who do not belong to the organization. Members can enter as many as they wish at no charge.

I also want to publicly thank all of the deer hunters who have shared their tales with me so I could write about them and allowed me the opportunity to photograph their trophy bucks. Extra appreciation goes out to the hunters who have allowed me to use photographs they have provided of their trophy whitetails. I never tire of hearing exciting deer tales, especially those dealing with big bucks, and seeing the trophy animals. An even bigger thanks goes out to family and friends who I have hunted with, sharing deer tales on another level.

My wife Lucy deserves special credit as my business partner who produced, designed and edited the book as well as took care of many of the other important details and work required to complete this book. Her skill and foresight as a business manager have made me more efficient in my writing as well as looking after many important business and personal details so I can concentrate on one of my life's most important activities - DEER HUNTING!

Introduction

No other whitetail buck that has been bagged in Michigan has generated the interest and attention across North America that surrounds a huge 12-point typical that Mitch Rompola from Traverse City collected with bow and arrow on November 13, 1998, and it's easy to understand why. Those impressively unique antlers grown by that deer officially score more than the current world record. The fact that Rompola spent three years trying to connect on that particular buck and missed a shot at the whitetail before finally getting it, adds to the story's appeal.

What really multiplies the intrigue is that the hunter who got this very special deer is as unique as the buck and even more mysterious. In order for a whitetail to be classified as a world record, its antlers must be entered into records compiled by the Pope and Young and/or the Boone and Crockett Clubs. The deer does not qualify for archery records maintained by Pope and Young because it was shot with a compound bow that has more than 65 percent letoff in draw weight at full draw.

If anyone else had taken that deer, they would register the rack with Boone and Crockett to claim the world record, but not Rompola. He said from the beginning that he had no intention of doing that, which is no surprise because he hasn't entered either of the other two sets of antlers from bucks he bagged that qualify for entry in B&C records. However, I don't think Rompola realized what a negative backlash his decision would cause. It has led to endless speculation about the legitimacy of the kill.

When the facts surrounding the case are considered, however, there can be no question about the authenticity of the Rompola buck. I've been asked countless times what I think about that whitetail and the hunter who took it, as have many other people. My answers are included in this book's first two chapters. Something that someone else wrote, which can be found at the end of chapter 3, is also applicable to the Rompola buck.

And there's an unavoidable connection to still one more chapter in this book. Chapter 14 is about senior citizen Jack Eddy, who has 22 bucks in state records, all taken with firearms. He commonly takes two book bucks per year and he put a friend of his onto a typical buck that should have netted in excess of 200. I haven't heard of anyone questioning Eddy's success, nor should they. But if Eddy can do it, why not Rompola?

Although chapters 1 and 2 cover what is probably Michigan's greatest deer tale of all time, the remaining 13 chapters are devoted to some impressive deer tales as well from all over the state. Chapter 8, for instance, is connected to discussion about world record whitetails. The current world record typical was shot by Milo Hanson in Saskatchewan. One of Michigan's highest scoring typicals was shot by another man named Hanson, which is discussed in that chapter.

Other chapters are devoted to a father and son who shared a hunt on which that year's biggest buck was bagged, a 14-year-old who got a world class whitetail during his first firearms hunt, a woman whose husband helped her bag a state record buck, a bowhunter who bagged a booner on his first hunt and much, much more. If you like this book, you should also enjoy books 1 and 2. Each of those books are filled with similar tales about how, where and when some of the state's biggest bucks were bagged.

Mitch Rompola from Traverse City graced the cover of the Winter 1999 issue of Buck Fax with the awesome 12-pointer he arrowed on the morning of November 13, 1998 that scored 216 5/8. Although the antlers have been examined and measured, they haven't been entered in state or national records.

Chapter 1

The Rompola Buck

A typical 12-pointer from Michigan that was taken with bow and arrow by Mitch Rompola from Traverse City on November 13, 1998 at 7:47 a.m., scores more than the current world record whitetail shot in Saskatchewan by Milo Hanson with a rifle during 1993. Hanson's 14-pointer had a final official score of 213 5/8.

The Rompola buck grossed 220 6/8 and netted 216 5/8, with an inside spread of 30 1/8 inches, according to Boone and Crockett measurer Gary Berger from Houghton Lake. Berger is also a measurer for state record keeper Commemorative Bucks of Michigan (CBM). The one-of-a-kind rack was panel measured for entry in state records on March 25, 1999, but a score sheet signed by the hunter is necessary to complete the process. That final step had not been completed more than two years after the antlers were officially measured. Hopefully, that will change some day.

But the buck will probably never be officially declared a world record whitetail. The antlers would have to be entered in national records maintained by the Boone and Crockett Club for that to happen. Since the day Mitch arrowed the whitetail, he made it clear he had no intention of doing that, which came as no surprise to those who know him.

Rompola has killed two other whitetails with archery equipment that have B&C caliber racks. Neither of them were entered in national records. The veteran big buck hunter has been consistent by following the same course with his most recent B&C qualifier. In fact, Mitch signed an agreement that prohibits him from entering the antlers in B&C records until and if another typical whitetail surpasses the Hanson buck.

Some people claim that the reason Mitch signed that agreement by a company representing the Hanson buck is there's something shady about the kill. In reality, the agreement simply reinforces his own intentions from the beginning. Beyond that, the agreement Rompola signed eliminated all speculation about his plans for the deer and

Rompola with another high scoring 12-pointer he bagged with bow and arrow in 1985. The antlers from this deer scored 181 7/8 and were entered in state records. It is the current state record typical bow kill, according to Commemorative Bucks of Michigan. Photo courtesy Mitch Rompola.

effectively removed the spotlight from him and his world class whitetail, which is also what he wanted.

The only thing Mitch does with the most consistency is arrow mature bucks with big racks. The enormous 12-pointer from '98 was reportedly the 21st whitetail he tagged that had antlers large enough to exceed bow and arrow big game record keeper Pope and Young minimums. Typical antlers have to measure a minimum of 125 to qualify for P&Y listing and nontypicals have to score at least 150.

Although the racks from many of the whitetails Mitch arrowed qualify for listing in Pope and Young Records, he has no more interest in having his deer listed in national bowhunting records than those maintained by the Boone and Crockett Club. Since the awesome 12-point he bagged during '98 was taken with a bow that has more than 65 percent letoff at full draw, that disqualifies it for entry. Under equipment restrictions established by P&Y, only whitetails taken with bows that have a maximum of 65 percent letoff will be considered for entry.

To finish out his hunting for 1998, Rompola bagged still one more book buck, an 8-pointer that was projected to score in the 130s. He shot that buck during early December from the same tree stand where he got the 12. It was one of two mature bucks that Mitch passed up before getting the 12. The other one he let go was a 10-point that had a bigger rack than the 8.

Rompola has entered a number of the trophy bucks he's bagged in state records, including another 12-pointer he tagged during 1985 that surpasses B&C minimums. Those antlers measured 181 7/8 and currently rank as Michigan's state record typical among bowhunters, according to CBM. He has 10 more bucks listed in state records besides the booner from 1985, all from Grand Traverse County.

For years, Mitch was Records Chairman for CBM, so he is very familiar with how antlers are measured and record keeping systems. Since most of his book bucks were taken in Michigan, he was satisfied with entering them in state records. That is, until 1988. Mitch stopped entering deer in state records by 1988 due to endless rumors about his phenomenal success.

Some hunters couldn't believe he was taking so many big bucks legally, although there was never any evidence to the contrary and there still isn't. He simply got tired of the constant, baseless, innuendos, figuring the nonsense would stop if there was no public record of him continuing his string of bowhunting success. And he was right.

After all, Rompola wasn't such an intense big buck hunter to make other people happy or the recognition that went with it. The challenge of outwitting mature bucks is what he lived for, so he continued, quietly, doing what he loved to do. Mitch also resigned as Records Chairman for CBM, concerned that rumors about him were negatively impacting the organization.

Although most of Mitch's book bucks have come from Michigan, his first ones were taken in his home state of Missouri. That's where he got his first booner, a 16-point nontypical that he arrowed when he was 14 years old. That rack scored 208 6/8.

Rompola readily admits there was a lot of luck involved in the taking of his first B&C qualifier many years ago. That's not the case with the 12-pointer from 1998. He pursued that whitetail for three years before finally getting it. The shaft that brought the buck down was actually the second arrow Mitch released at the deer. His first shot, taken on November 3rd, missed when it was deflected.

September of 1996 was when Rompola got his first good look at the impressive whitetail, although he had gotten a glimpse of it the year before. He had permission to

Mitch shot his whopper whitetail during 1998 while hunting from a tree stand. He has taken many trophy bucks from the ground.

hunt the parcel of private property where he saw the deer. Once Mitch saw what an outstanding specimen the whitetail was, he set out to learn as much as he could about the animal's movements to determine where he might be able to ambush it.

He quickly learned the buck's rack wasn't the only thing distinctive about it. The deer's right front hoof had a blemish that was easy to identify. That gave the bowhunter an important advantage because he didn't have to actually see the animal to know where it had been. Its tracks clued him in to its travel routes and favored haunts.

Mitch set up a mock scrape that the buck began visiting, but the monster wasn't the only antlered whitetail that took to the scrape. Another adult buck with an impressive set of headgear also claimed that turf. Rompola could have shot the long-tined 10-pointer near the mock scrape on opening day of the 1996 bow season (October 1), but he passed him up to wait for the wider-antlered whitetail.

That 10 had a bigger rack than any other whitetail he had ever let go, but he figured it was important to increase his chances of connecting on the 12. He didn't know it at the time, but if he had killed that buck on October 1, he might have been putting his second tag on the bigger whitetail October 12, 1996. The buck with the massive 12-point rack was approaching the scrape on the 12th, as Mitch watched from his tree stand, when the aggressive whitetail he spared 11 days earlier, rushed in and chased it away.

Angry that the buck with the narrower rack had cost him the chance he had been waiting months for and concerned that the 10-point might injure the 12 during a future fight, Rompola decided to do what he then realized he should have done on October 1. Taking advantage of the 10-pointer's tendency to defend the scrape from other bucks, Mitch used a call made by Fred and Greg Abbas in Michigan and grunted to lure it into position for a bow shot. It's hard to imagine being disappointed about bow-bagging a whitetail with antlers that score a little more than 168, but Rompola was to some extent that day.

However, he soon got over it, knowing there was still an opportunity to get the biggest buck of his career. But that opportunity didn't come during the remainder of 1996 or '97. Mitch continued monitoring the whitetail's movements and he saw it occasionally.

He spotted the buck in a bed during July of '97, for instance, when its antlers were still developing, but their paths didn't cross once bow season opened. So Rompola settled for a 150 class 13-pointer during October of that year. With one tag filled, Mitch moved to a ground blind one evening where he found the most recent sign from the 12-pointer.

The effort paid off in terms of another sighting. Even though the wide-antlered whitetail came within 30 yards, there was no chance for a good bow shot. However, Mitch got a better idea of exactly how wide the deer's rack was as a result of that encounter. While observing the buck, Rompola took note of a pair of branches each beam touched at the same time. Later measurement of the distance between those branches came up with a figure of 34 inches.

Mitch saw the buck once more during the last week of December in 1997 at a distance of about 30 yards again, but no shot was possible then either. The circumstances were a little different that time. The whitetail caught Rompola by surprise when it appeared suddenly as he was ready to call it quits after a morning sit.

There was snow on the ground and Mitch had snuck into a ground blind quietly that was in the deer's bedding area. After waiting for 2 1/2 hours without seeing anything, the archer took the arrow from his string and put it in his quiver. He had removed the quiver from his bow when he reached the blind. As he reattached the quiver to his bow, the corresponding sound caused the buck that Mitch had been waiting for to stand up from its bed 30 yards away. It had been there the entire time behind a blowdown.

Rompola knew it would be impossible to put an arrow back on the string for a shot, but he had the piece of mind to focus his camera on the whitetail as it stared at him and snapped one photograph before the deer walked off. Although he didn't have the buck, he had proof of its existence.

By 1998, the exceptional buck seemed to disappear. Mitch didn't see the deer or any of its distinctive tracks during the summer through most of October. He was concerned it had moved out of the area for good or was dead. However, as October was winding down, Rompola finally saw the whitetail as it crossed a woods road, much to his relief.

Mitch later found out that the buck had been spending most of its time in another area where at least one other hunter saw it and tried to take it with bow and arrow. Pressure from that hunter caused the whitetail to move back to the portion of its territory where Rompola had encountered it previously.

On November 3rd, Mitch saw the buck again. This time he was in his tree stand with his bow and arrows. He described what happened then during an interview on the Michigan Out-of-Doors Television Show with cohost James Ford.

"That evening, he came back into another scrape off one of my other stand sites. I took a photo of him standing in the scrape. He's looking away from me. When you see the photo, it just scares you.

"Well, the minute I took the photo, he started walking over towards me. So I put the camera down, of course. I didn't want to be dinking around with that. He comes right over to me and stands there; I figured about 20 yards or so.

"I shot and he took three great big bounds. Of course, everything happens real quick you know, when you're shaking anyway. I couldn't believe I was shaking. I was watching him and thought, 'My gosh, what happened here?'"

"He started wagging his tail and that's when I knew I missed him."

"Now what do you owe that miss to," Ford asked.

"Well, not to make any excuses," Rompola continued, "but I hit some brush. The arrow caught some brush. He was in some ferns. Actually, I was trying to heart shoot

The Rompola Buck

The 12-point Mitch tagged in 1985 that is shown here was 4 1/2 years old. If it had lived another 3 years, its antlers may have rivaled the whitetail Rompola killed in 1998. There are similarities between the racks.

him, so I shot a hair low. It caught something and put the arrow right underneath him.

"He really never knew what happened. Luckily, I didn't wound him or touch him. He just walked away. I knew I missed him, but I didn't know exactly what happened when I went down and got my arrow. It was sticking almost straight up in the ground."

In another television interview with Dan Boss from Traverse City, who cohosts a show called "Hook and Hunting," Mitch commented about the miss: "There were a few days there that I was pretty sick about it, to say the least. I thought I had my one opportunity, my one chance in a lifetime at him. I was, of course, hoping to get another one. As it turned out, I did. I was fortunate."

Rompola got his second chance at the world class buck on the morning of November 13th, but he also saw him on the evening of the 12th. The 8 and 10-point bucks that were also using the mock scrape showed up first. While they were near the scrape, they looked up a nearby ridge like they heard or saw something and left. The 12-pointer soon appeared from the direction the other bucks had been looking and disappeared along the same route they had taken into a thick swamp filled with cedar and tag alder trees.

Mitch was in another tree stand about 100 yards away before daylight the next morning. About an hour later, the same 8 and 10-point bucks he saw the evening before, walked by 12 yards away. The buck that Rompola was waiting for was right behind them.

"They no sooner disappeared and here he come," Mitch told James Ford. "I was all ready for him actually because the two bucks had gotten me ready. I was up and ready. Here he come and I thought, ' Man, I'm not going to miss you this time.' He come by this one tree that blinds him from me and as soon as he got behind that I drew.

"He got out there - it was actually 11 yards - a little angled away, just a beautiful shot. I didn't get cocky. I center shot him. The arrow went in him real nice. It stayed in him. Hit him in the right front shoulder and he took off.

"I sat down because I was going to fall out of that tree if I didn't. I sat there for a while and thought, 'I really did it! I really did it!' You visualize this so many times you wonder. I looked at my quiver and said 'Yup, there's an arrow missing.'"

Mitch got his composure back in about 15 minutes and climbed out of the tree. He went to his truck and drove home to get his video camera.

"When I recovered the deer I kept the camera running the whole time," Mitch commented. "I never turned the camera off. I videoed the entire recovery. It all happened on Friday the 13th. Now that's my lucky day!"

The video is important documentation of the authenticity of the kill. The rumors and suspicions Rompola had put up with in the past about other bucks he had taken made him realize the value of documenting this very special whitetail. After he got the buck home, he also invited a conservation officer for the Grand Traverse Band of Ottawa and Chippewa Indians - Bill Bailey from Honor - to see the deer while it was intact. Bailey is a friend of Rompola's and he knew about the bowhunter's quest for the whitetail. Nonetheless, it was important for some one with Bailey's credentials to see the buck and verify there was nothing suspicious about the kill.

There's more documentation of the legitimacy of the Rompola buck than most other world class whitetails that have been taken in North America. Inspite of this, some people continue to question the kill. It's amazing how easy it is for some hunters to ignore reality in the presence of plenty of facts.

Mitch showed the buck to a number of other people, too, just like any hunter would who took such an amazing whitetail. However, Rompola is not like most other deer hunters in many respects and he should not be judged as though he is. After all, few, if any, others have tagged a trio of Boone and Crockett bucks with bow and arrow. And he's the only bowhunter on record with a typical buck to his credit that nets more than 210.

The enormous typical was aged at 7 1/2 years old. It had a dressed weight of 263 pounds. The 12-point scoring 181 7/8 that Mitch shot in 1985 was 4 1/2 years old and had similar antler features to the buck from 1998. If it had lived another three years, it might have grown a rack to rival the one that has captured the attention of most whitetail hunters since the fall of 1998.

The story about Mitch Rompola doesn't end in 1998. He continues to hunt and consistently take mature whitetail bucks with bow and arrow. He arrowed a 9-pointer during the fall of 1999 that scored in the 140s. Rompola bagged a pair of 10-pointers during 2000, one of which was taken in the Upper Peninsula. The U.P. buck also scored in the 140s. A 10-point he tagged in Grand Traverse County measured in the 150s.

You might be hearing more about the enormous 12-pointer he got during '98 in the future. And I wouldn't be the least bit surprised if Mitch connects on another booner. Stay tuned.

For more reading about Mitch Rompola and how he hunts, refer to a copy of Book 1 of <u>Great Michigan Deer Tales</u>. One of the chapters in that book includes more details about how he hunts and has anecdotes about how he bagged other big bucks, including the 12-point scoring 181 7/8 that he got during 1985 and another one he missed on his first chance before getting it with a second arrow a week later.

Mitch Rompola and his now famous buck were published on the cover of the March 1999 issue of Woods-N-Water News. The first installment of a 2-part story about Rompola's 3-year quest for the exceptional whitetail was also published in this issue of the magazine.

Chapter 2

Rompola Continued

What should have been a joyous accomplishment for Mitch Rompola, a reason for pride among Michigan deer hunters and a feather in the cap of North American whitetail hunting has turned out to be a nightmare for Rompola. Mitch did get to enjoy the euphoria that must accompany the bagging of one of the most awesome whitetail bucks on the continent for a brief period of time, until it was taken away from him by the dark side of deer hunting. The baseless skepticism and negativity, fueled solely by unfounded rumor, surrounding Rompola's tremendous accomplishment was so strong, it stole something very precious from all of us, not just Mitch Rompola.

When the dark side of deer hunting can successfully raise doubts about the legitimacy of a whopper of a whitetail that was taken legally, we all lose. When the entering of a set of antlers in state and/or national records, no matter how exceptional, becomes mandatory in many hunters' eyes, instead of voluntary, before it can be accepted by the public, we've lost sight of what deer hunting is about. The same thing is true when the individual sense of accomplishment that goes with a successful hunt is lost or taken away in the rush to define what the hunt does or does not mean to others.

There's now a dark cloud of uncertainty in many hunters' minds hanging over the Rompola buck that shouldn't be there. If doubts about the Rompola buck can be successfully raised inspite of the steps that Mitch took to document his kill, which were above and beyond what most hunters who have shot world class bucks would do and have done, the same thing can happen to anyone anywhere. The controversy surrounding the one-of-a-kind Michigan typical that Rompola arrowed on November 13, 1998 clearly confirms that the word of the lone hunter is suspect no matter how legally and ethically a hunt was carried out. And the vast majority of North American whitetail hunters are by themselves when they score.

As a result of the rumors that surround the Rompola buck and the intense scrutiny he and the deer received, other hunters who bag super bucks in the future might be

Mitch Rompola with the head mount of the Boone and Crockett class nontypical he arrowed in Missouri as a teenager. The antlers score 208 6/8. Mitch's first bow kill was a 9-pointer measuring 151 that he got when he was 9 years old.

discouraged from going public with their kills. As an outdoor writer, I hope that doesn't happen, but I wouldn't be surprised if it does. I know of at least one hunter who bagged a megabuck in Michigan since Rompola got his, who refused to go public because he didn't want all of the attention associated with it and I can't blame him. Although I would have liked writing an article about his hunt, I respected his wishes. Some members of the media are not willing to do that.

I can only guess that a lot of the assumptions, speculation and rumors surrounding the Rompola buck are based on limited information as well as pure skepticism. If any whitetail hunter was capable of setting out to claim a world record buck with bow and arrow and succeeding, Mitch is certainly among the few who qualify. Afterall, he's been setting records while bowhunting for whitetails since he was 9 years old in Missouri.

Rompola grew up on a farm in Missouri with his family before moving to Michigan at the age of 18 when he joined the Coast Guard. He started bowhunting for whitetails in 1958 at the age of 9 with a 50 pound pull Ben Pearson recurve bow. He arrowed a trophy 9-pointer that year that was the highest scoring typical bow kill on record for the state with a score of 151. He ambushed the buck from a hollowed out muskrat house that served as his blind.

Four years later, he connected on his first Boone and Crockett Class whitetail, a 16-point nontypical that scored 208 6/8. That buck was a Missouri state record among nontypical bow kills. Mitch readily admits more luck than skill was involved in making that kill, but that has been the exception rather than the rule.

It was the late 1960s when Mitch moved to Michigan. He nailed a buck that measured 105 5/8 during 1968 and another whitetail that scored 145 3/8 in 1969, but it took him years to learn the habits and habitat of mature bucks near his new home to the point where he could take them consistently. That started happening by the early 1980s.

Rompola bagged an 11-pointer during 1982 that scored 161 and then in 1985 he collected an impressive 12-point with a typical rack measuring 181 7/8. That was his first booner with typical antlers that has been a state record bow kill in that category ever since. Mitch didn't enter that deer in B&C records and I don't recall any negative fallout because of it.

However, there were people who questioned Mitch's ability to consistently take quality bucks then as there are now. A letter to the editor of Buck Fax, which is Commemorative Bucks of Michigan's (CBM) quarterly magazine, to that effect that was written by Dar Van Den Bosch from Zeeland, was published in the Spring 1991 issue.

"You should look into the 11 entries of Mitch Rompola," he wrote. "It is impossible for one man to be so successful shooting so many big bucks. Do you know all of the things that must go right to just get one big buck in your life? Nobody is that lucky over and over again."

Mr. Van Den Bosch was correct in stating that nobody can be LUCKY enough to take 11 book bucks. However, some hunters are SKILLFUL and PERSISTENT enough

Rompola with 15-pointer scoring 146 7/8 that he got during November of 1984. He missed this whitetail with an arrow 11 days before he scored on it. Circumstances were similar during his hunt for the one-of-a-kind buck in 1998. Photo courtesy Mitch Rompola.

to consistently tag bucks with high scoring racks. It takes a lot of time, effort and dedication to be as successful as Mitch has been, plus some luck once in a while.

Rompola is indeed a unique deer hunter, but there are other hunters who have more whitetail heads in both state and national records than Mitch does. No, it's not easy, but it's not impossible either. We should try to learn from these knowledgeable individuals rather than criticize them for being so successful. I don't know many whitetail hunters who wouldn't mind having as many book bucks to their credit as Mitch does. The fact that most don't reflects the difficulty involved in doing so.

Mitch was Records Chairman for CBM during 1991 and his response to the letter writer was also printed:

> *Unfortunately, Mr. Van Den Bosh has chosen to make inaccurate assumptions about me and my hunting success without having met me or knowing anything about me. He's not the first to have done this. Why do people insist on making accusations based on ignorance?*
>
> *I do not rely on luck to take big bucks. Many years of research and experience go into my hunting success. I was studying whitetails before I was a teenager and I now have over 30 years of research and observations about their habits and habitat behind me.*
>
> *Over the past 16 years, I have thoroughly mapped over six square miles of my hunting areas to show the way deer utilize their range. I have backtracked hundreds of miles of runways, learning travel routines, feeding areas and bedding locations.*
>
> *I know all of the preferred and available food sources used at any time of the year. I know how the variations in weather alter their travel patterns. I know how the deer change their travel and bedding routines with the change in food supplies from fall through spring.*
>
> *I know to the day when major scrape lines are opened from year-to-year. I know when the majority of the mature does will be bred and how many yearling does are in the areas and when they will be ready to be bred. I know what bucks have survived hunting seasons through post season scouting.*
>
> *When most hunters have quit thinking about deer hunting at the end of the season, I will be preparing for the next season. I spend the winter months scouting and mapping buck routines, setting up new stands and cutting approach trails to them. I also cut cedar to feed deer through the winter.*
>
> *My hunting scheme is calculated. The areas I select and my approach into them are precisely planned. By the time the hunting season arrives, I will have put in more time preparing for it than most hunters will spend hunting. By the end of the season, I will have used over 40 different stand sites.*
>
> *I have taken my hunting to such an extreme level that it would boggle the minds of most hunters. The knowledge that I have obtained on whitetail deer*

behavior would rival that of any biologist or deer expert in this country. All my observations are made on deer in their natural environment, not enclosures. All of my experiences are first hand, not from something I have read or been told or seen on a video.

For over 30 years I have kept a hunting journal on my studies and observations. Data taken from the past 10 years shows that if I could have taken every big buck I had in bow range, I would have over 50 in the records. From the last 10 years I have seen 68 big bucks, 56 of which were in bow range. I managed to take 10 of those.

As far as knowing what it takes and what must go right to take a big buck, there isn't anyone who hunts deer that knows this any better than I do. In fact, I could add many more things that can go wrong, most of which are controllable mistakes. I eliminate as much human error from my hunting as possible. I take control of the situation and put the luck factor in my favor. All of my shots are set up for 20 yards or less.

I have tracked hundreds of bow-shot deer. I will track and recover more deer in a single season than most hunters do in their lives. Every season I recover many deer for other hunters that they had given up on. My sons are also expert trackers and have assisted me many times.

My entries have been investigated many times, mostly by anti-hunting groups that would like to discredit me. I have witnesses to all of my deer. Some witnesses were hunting with me at the time I scored and others helped me get the deer out of the woods.

Many people have also seen these deer alive. There were over a dozen people who had seen my state record deer from 1985 alive, two from an airplane. I have pictures of all of my deer.

I am also not the only one taking big bucks out of these areas. Last season, six record book bucks were taken by other hunters. One bow kill scored over 160 typical.

Everyone hunts at their own level. It's like anything one does. You get out of it what you put into it.

All most people see are my end results - a picture of my deer or my name in the records. Yet most can't begin to comprehend the time and effort to accomplish what I have achieved. What I have written here is a very brief explanation of what I have done to put the odds in my favor. Does this sound like a hunter who has put 11 entries into the records by hunting on luck?

Critical comments like the one above, and there were others, are why Rompola stopped entering his kills in state records after 1988. But he continued hunting and taking big bucks. That remained one of his passions. He didn't need to justify his success to anyone. In fact, he grew tired of dealing with hunters who simply didn't get it.

For the record, there were other hunters who took trophy bucks from Grand Traverse County. Another Boone and Crockett qualifier was shot in the county during the 1976 firearms season by Jim Thomson. He bagged a 12-pointer that scored 174 5/8. Richard Barrett claimed a 10-point in the county with a firearm during 1991 that measured 152, according to CBM records. The 1993 gun hunt produced a 12-point for Steven B. Johnson that tallied 150 6/8.

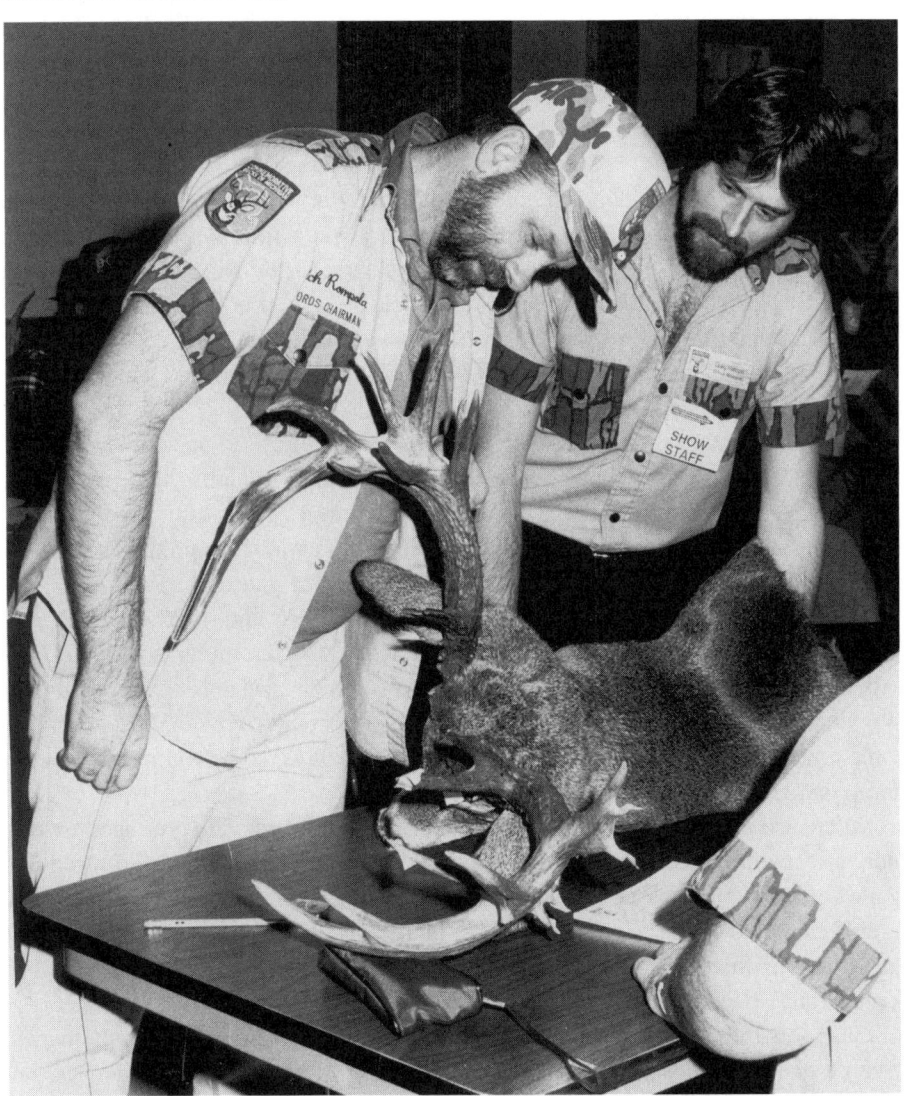

Because of Mitch's long affiliation with CBM as Records Chairman, he permitted the organization to publish photographs and a story about his remarkable hunt. Rompola is shown checking on the measuring of a nontypical rack in this photograph at the Michigan Deer Spectacular when he was Records Chairman.

Although some hunters failed to understand Rompola's phenomenal success, many did. An article I wrote about Mitch's whitetail hunting accomplishments was published in the August 1986 issue of Outdoor Life Magazine, giving him national exposure. Plenty of hunters wanted to benefit from his knowledge, which prompted him to begin public speaking, primarily at shows and banquets in Michigan.

Mitch and I were both speakers at the Michigan Deer Spectacular in Lansing during February of 1993. At the time, he was patterning a trophy buck that he hoped to take during the upcoming fall. He had spent a lot of time following the whitetail's tracks in the snow, both forwards and backwards. He had managed to take at least one good photograph of the buck before it lost its antlers and he picked up one of its sheds.

I saw the photograph and shed along with many other hunters who attended that show. Based on the information Rompola had gathered about the deer, he figured its antlers would score close to 200. As the 1994 season was drawing to a close, I called Mitch to find out how he had done on the buck he was after. As it turns out, that whitetail escaped him.

The deer disappeared. Mitch didn't know if it had been hit by a vehicle when it was antlerless or it had been poached. He simply lost track of it.

I point this out to show that Rompola doesn't get all of the bucks he's after. No hunter does. It's also further evidence of the caliber of whitetails the areas he hunts are capable of producing and the effort Mitch is willing to go to, to try to get them. If there was a buck as big or bigger than the one that got away, Rompola is the one who was bound to know about it and stand the best chance of getting it.

The well documented chain of events between 1996 and 1998 covered in the previous chapter that led to him claiming the enormous 12-pointer scoring 216 5/8, confirms that. Although Mitch was no longer Records Chairman for CBM by then, he maintained regular contact with officers and measurers who were good friends. These people understood what an exceptional hunter Rompola is, so he routinely shared his hunting experiences with them.

Mitch also confided in local television reporter Dan Boss, who produces a weekly outdoor segment called "Hook and Hunting" for Channels 9 &10. Mitch told these people about the big buck he was hunting over the course of the three years it took him to get it. I talked to many of Rompola's friends as well as Boss and they confirmed that. Some of them had seen photos of the buck when it was alive that Mitch had taken during December of 1997 and November 3, 1998.

I also saw those photographs and there's no doubt the whitetail in those images is the same one he killed. Gary Berger from Houghton Lake is one of Mitch's friends who he told about his quest for the outstanding whitetail. Berger is a measurer for CBM as well as Boone and Crockett. Gary is one of three CBM scorers who eventually measured the Rompola buck. He saw and handled the antlers and was able to inspect them on the skull plate.

There's no question in Berger's mind about the reality of what Mitch accomplished.

"I can tell you right now that the story is authentic," Gary said. "The truth of the matter is it's an authentic bow kill. Mitch is strictly a trophy hunter. He told me three years ago that if he got that buck it could be bigger than the present world record.

"He didn't get the buck during 1997 because his job interfered. He quit his job in 1998 to increase his chances of getting it and he managed to pull it off. He was hunting on private land that butts up to state land. The buck was actually bedding in a big swamp on state land."

Rompola has been accused of being secretive about the deer, refusing to show it to anyone after he got it. That simply isn't true. He went the extra mile to document the kill because he knew what he had. Mitch video-taped the entire recovery of the whitetail from his tree stand to where it went down.

After the buck was loaded in his truck, he excitedly shared his success with friends and relatives who knew about the buck. One of those friends is a conservation officer - Bill Bailey from Honor. If Rompola had anything to hide, he certainly wouldn't have let an officer inspect the whitetail.

And Bailey did look at the deer closely. He handled the carcass and antlers. In numerous interviews, Bailey confirmed that there was nothing suspicious about the buck. It's antlers certainly hadn't been tampered with. That's something that would have been easy to see.

Because of Mitch's previous long affiliation with CBM, the organization's magazine - Buck Fax - was one of the first to publish a story and photos of the deer. Mitch wrote an account of what happened after the kill for the publication. After shooting the buck that he had worked so hard for, Mitch went home to give his girlfriend the news, get a plastic drag that enables him to move big bucks by himself and to get his cameras.

> *I quickly grabbed my deer drag, cameras and two quick pieces of toast. I hadn't eaten breakfast and had to have something to sustain me because moving the buck was going to require hours of grueling uphill dragging, which it did. The toast was all I had to eat until the next day.*
>
> *I jumped in the truck and hurried back to the spot where I shot the buck. My previous truck tracks were the only ones in or out. I felt good. I knew the buck was probably down because the shot was so good.*
>
> *When I got to the stand site, I climbed back into my stand, turned the video camera on and video taped the scene. I came down out of the stand and tracked the deer through the camera lens all the way to the deer. The camera was never turned off from the stand to the recovery. My comments are all on the tape. The buck was awesome.*
>
> *After I got the buck in the truck, I took the deer to show my girlfriend and let her know I was okay. From there, I took the film in for one hour processing.*

The deer was in the back of the truck. While waiting for the photos to be processed, I drove to several friends' houses to show them the deer.

After an hour, I went back and got the pictures, then went home to change clothes. I was so excited, I drove to Kevin Kreh's house in Manton. He had a house full of relatives and they all poured out to see the deer. It was great!

From there, I drove to Gary Berger's home in Houghton Lake. He wasn't home, so I assumed he had left for the U.P. for the opener of the firearms deer season. Disappointed, I left for home, not knowing that Gary had only gone to town and returned about a half hour after I left. Boy, was he disappointed.

Even though it was late, when I got back to Traverse City, I drove over to Cliff's Rifle Shop, but Cliff wasn't there either. I knew these guys wanted to see the deer because they all knew I had been after him for several years.

It was now so late in the evening that I returned home and steered the truck into the garage. Too exhausted to eat, I went into the house and collapsed on the bed until morning.

The parade began soon after I woke up. Kevin Kreh had called a number of his friends, they called their friends and so forth. Word was out. Soon, there were lots of people, friends and strangers alike, coming and going like ants wanting to see the deer. It was crazy. At times the driveway was full of vehicles and many more were parked up and down the street.

Strangers that had seen the deer returned with more strangers. Between the phone in the house and people in the yard, I was busy running back and forth. That night, I took the deer to show more friends. On the way home, I stopped at Cliff's Rifle Shop again, but he still wasn't around.

Back to the house again where I called Bill Bailey, an 18-year veteran tribal conservation officer. I refer to the Bailey Family as the Benoits of Michigan. They are an uncanny bunch of serious deer hunters who have shot many big bucks. Bill also knew I'd been after this deer and exploded with excitement when I told him I got it.

He said, "I'll be there in 20 minutes!"

A few minutes after Bill showed up, two more car loads of Baileys and friends drove in. What fun! These guys really knew a good trophy when they saw one.

The next day, Sunday, I tried calling my friend Dan Boss, a reporter for local television station TV 9&10. For the past two years, Dan was aware that I was pursing the big buck and had seen the picture of it that I had taken in the wild. Unfortunately, Dan was out of town hunting near Charlevoix. This was the opening day of the firearms deer season. His wife called where he was staying and left a message for him.

Dan got the message and called me that night. Because he's so good with a camera, I really wanted him to get the deer on film or video before I had to *process it. Dan said he would be unable to get back here for at least another day or so. Regrettably, I had to skin the buck and partly process it that day because it had already lain in the truck too long.*

By Monday afternoon, the phone was ringing off the hook. A media feeding frenzy had begun. Reporters were besieging me from all over the country. I didn't know it at the time, but news of the deer, along with my address and phone number had been posted on the internet. The phone rang through the night.

On Tuesday, I received a welcome call from Dan Boss. He came over and did a segment for the local news. Contrary to what's been told, he's the only media person I've ever contacted. I received over 100 additional calls that day. That night, I pulled the plug on the outside phone box.

Wednesday morning, I plugged it back in and had over 60 calls by 11:00 a.m. The phone was killing me and it looked like it. Everybody wanted a piece of me, so on that day I had my number disconnected. I didn't want all of this attention and still don't. I just wanted to share the deer with my good friends and a few interested people.

People are adamantly insisting that I must do certain things to get the buck entered in the record books. Well, I'm not interested in the record books, but I'm still fascinated by the antler measurements for comparison among my personal racks. The record books used to be important to me, but they're not anymore.

Although I've shot a good number of trophy bucks in recent years, I haven't entered any of them since 1988. For now, don't expect this one to be treated any differently. It may be entered someday, or it may not.

Antlers from the Rompola buck had been green scored when the 1999 winter issue of Buck Fax was published. The green gross score was 223 and the rack netted 218 5/8. Mitch knew there would be a lot of interest in the whitetail he arrowed and there would be skeptics, but he dramatically underestimated how overwhelming the reaction would be. Release of information about the deer and hunter on the internet contributed to the rapid speed that so many people found out about what happened.

Rompola did his best to get the true story about his success out to the public. He did the television interview with Dan Boss that aired on November 19, 1998 and he also did at least two more television interviews. One was for the Michigan Out-of-Doors Television Show that aired on public stations in the state on November 28. The other was with Denny Geurink for his weekly outdoor television show that aired November 29. Mitch supplied some of his video of the recovery of the deer for those programs. He also did numerous newspaper and magazine interviews, providing photographs of him with the buck where it fell.

Dan Bertalan from Lansing did an in depth interview with Mitch that resulted in a two-part series for Michigan magazine Woods-N-Water News (March and April 1999 issues) and national magazine Deer & Deer Hunting (August and September 1999 issues). Gordon Charles from Traverse City wrote an article for the April 1999 issue of Michigan Hunting & Fishing Magazine. Other writers were also able to interview Rompola and wrote accurate accounts.

Due to family health problems, official measuring of the Rompola buck was delayed until late March, more than 120 days after the whitetail was taken. The panel of measurers included Gary Berger, Al Brown from Kalkaska and Lee Holbrook from Boyne Falls. The trio came up with an official net score of 216 5/8 and a gross score of 220 6/8. The beams were similar in length to the inside spread - around 30 inches - and the longest tines measured about 14 inches.

Some of the skeptics questioned whether Michigan was/is capable of producing a buck with antlers of that caliber. I beg your pardon! Just two years before Rompola scored on his awesome whitetail, Troy Stephens shot a 16-pointer in Jackson County that grossed 214 3/8 as a typical. After 16 3/8 inches of deductions, the rack ended up netting 198. If those antlers had been more symmetrical, they would have netted well over 200.

There were only about six inches difference between the gross scores of both bucks and the Stephens buck was thought to be 5 1/2 years old. Imagine what that

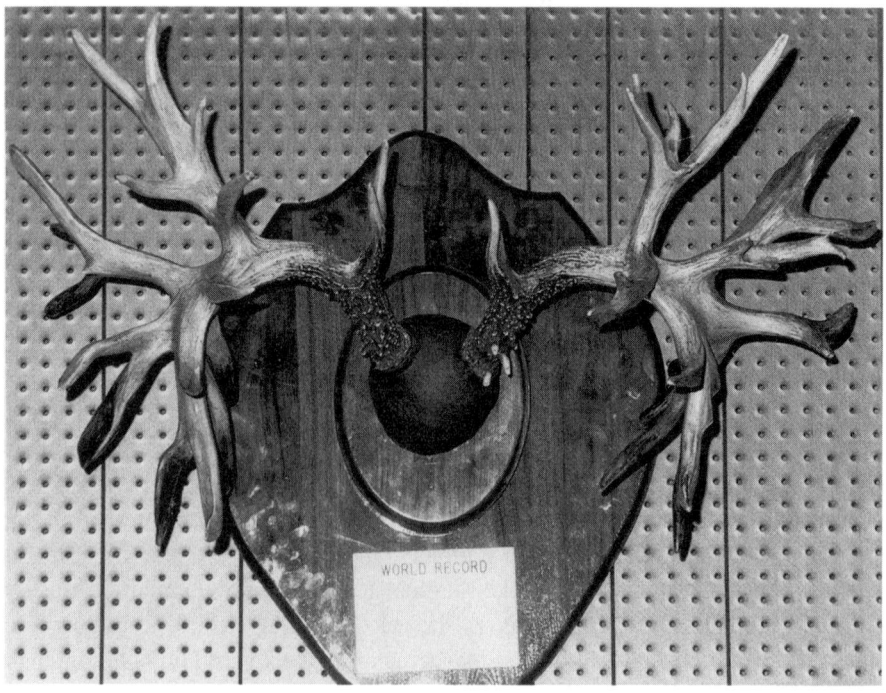

Whitetail bucks with world class antlers are excellent at avoiding hunters. The deer that grew this world record nontypical rack was found dead in St. Louis County, Missouri on November 15, 1981. The antlers measured 333 7/8.

whitetail's antlers could have scored in another two years. A chapter in Book 2 of Great Michigan Deer Tales is devoted to the Stephens deer, complete with a score sheet for the antlers.

And it's no secret that world class whitetails are good at eluding hunters. That's why a pair of bucks with the highest scoring nontypical racks known to exist died of accidental deaths in Missouri and Ohio. The carcasses of those deer were found, but it's a safe bet that other whitetails with some of the largest antlers in North America have died without any hunter ever seeing them dead or alive.

Other nonbelievers claim that Rompola killed the buck to make money. He certainly did make some money as a result of the kill, but he could have made much more by entering it in national records, taking the head on the show circuit as Milo Hanson has and expanding his public speaking opportunities. He could have also done major product endorsements. The fact that Mitch minimized the money making potential that his hunting success afforded him, is proof that was not important to him.

Inspite of Mitch's efforts and the reinforcing comments of the men who saw the deer and measured the antlers, confirming there is nothing suspicious about the circumstances or the rack, negative reaction persisted even though there was no basis in fact for any of it. For specific quotes from the measurers, refer to the September 1999 issues of North American Whitetail and Michigan Sportsman Magazines. Consequently, Rompola gave up dealing with the media and public and I can understand why. How would you feel if you finally succeeded in collecting the biggest whitetail in the world during a fair chase hunt after three years of effort and then found out many people didn't believe you, even though you documented the kill?

What should have been an overwhelmingly positive experience, remains in limbo and Rompola is not the only loser. All deer hunters have lost something, but few have lost as much as Mitch has, and his family has obviously been impacted, too. Although Rompola still has the personal satisfaction of knowing what he accomplished, he should also have the respect and admiration from the world of whitetail hunters. If the nay sayers can steal the sense of pride and accomplishment from him that he should feel when in public, they can do the same to anyone.

And the rest of us are deprived of the opportunity to see the super buck in person and marvel at its dimensions. Rompola had plans for public display of the whitetail when he got it. The rumor mongers caused a change in those plans. The dark side of deer hunting has taken more away from the sport than many people may realize.

The bottom line is that Mitch Rompola is sometimes as secretive, elusive and mysterious as the mature whitetail bucks he's so passionate about hunting. Those qualities in whitetails have earned the respect of most hunters. It shouldn't be any different how they view Rompola.

Esther Frantom with her state record muzzleloader buck among women. She shot the 10-pointer on November 17, 1998. The antlers measure 163. Photo courtesy Esther Frantom.

Chapter 3

Branch County Muzzleloader Records

Branch County has the unique distinction of producing state record bucks taken with muzzleloaders two years in a row. Esther Frantom from Ohio bagged the state record typical among women during 1998 and Brandon Dirschell from Coldwater collected the alltime state record nontypical black powder buck in 1999. Here are the stories behind these two exceptional whitetails.

One thing Esther Frantom likes about deer hunting with a muzzleloading rifle is there's little to no recoil compared to a shotgun. The fact that she used a front loader to take a trophy buck during the fall of 1998 doesn't hurt either. That big buck not only happened to be her best ever, the antlers from that whitetail had one of the largest typical racks known taken with a muzzleloader in the state during 1998 seasons, according to state record keeper Commemorative Bucks of Michigan (CBM).

CBM gives out annual awards for the biggest bucks taken by women as well as men to make sure both sexes get recognition for their accomplishments. Frantom shot a wide-racked 10-pointer in Branch County during the regular firearm season that had a final official score of 163.

Esther's deer is the highest scoring black powder buck with typical antlers on record for Branch County, according to CBM records. The rack was in the 11th spot on the list of alltime typical muzzleloader kills when this was written. I don't know of any hunter, male or female, who wouldn't be happy with a buck like that.

Esther got her book buck during the afternoon of November 17, 1998. Deer hunters in the state's southern counties are limited to using shotguns, muzzleloaders or handguns. Frantom chose a muzzleloader over a shotgun because of the light recoil. She borrowed her husband's .50 caliber Knight front loader to hunt with. It was loaded with a 240 grain bullet ahead of 90 grains of black powder. The rifle was fitted with a 3-9 power

Simmons scope.

Frantom's husband Doren was also kind enough to allow Esther to hunt from a spot where he normally waits for whitetails on the day she scored. Doren got his wife interested in hunting and was anxious for her to have a good time, see as many deer as possible and shoot one, if possible. The fall of '98 was Esther's second year of whitetail hunting. She bagged a button buck with a 20 gauge shotgun the year before.

Although Esther ended up tagging an antlerless buck during the fall of 1997, she did see a big buck during that hunt.

"As I sat quietly waiting and getting very impatient, I saw a big buck walking down a distant fenceline," she said. "I hoped he would turn, come my way and get into range, but no such luck. He kept walking until he was out of sight.

"Later that same day, a button buck came by in range, so I shot him. Everyone laughed and had their fun with me about how small he was, but they're not laughing anymore."

It was the last day of the first week of the season during '97 (November 21) when Esther shot the button buck. Most hunters are willing to take any legal deer by then, if they haven't filled a tag, and first time hunters are normally more anxious to score than those with experience. In Frantom's case, the young buck was sort of a birthday present. Her birthday is on November 22.

Esther and Doren live in Ohio, but Doren is originally from Branch County. They return to Michigan every fall to hunt with Doren's brother. Although 1997 was the first fall that Esther carried a gun while deer hunting, she accompanied her husband in the field the year before to watch and "learn the tricks of hunting." She obviously is a quick learner.

"On opening day of the 1998 season, I sat in a tree stand watching and waiting for some action," Esther said. "Finally, a 6-pointer came about 20 yards from my tree. I took my shot, but wouldn't you know it, all I could find was lots of fur, but no blood. I figured that was my last shot at a buck."

Frantom's shot just grazed the 6-point and she was understandably disappointed about missing her chance at an antlered buck. She couldn't know it at the time, but it was a good thing that whitetail got away. She might not have still been hunting by the third day of the season if she had bagged it.

There was a lot of deer activity within view of Esther on November 15, 1998. Besides missing the 6-point, Esther saw no less than 75 deer from her stand on opening day of gun season. One of those whitetails was a big buck, but, like the year before, it was too far away for a shot. A second 6-point that was out of range was among the deer she saw.

Action then dropped off until the afternoon of the third day. After seeing so many deer on the first day of hunting, Esther was optimistic about a repeat performance, but it wasn't to be. However, she still remained confident about getting a deer and resumed hunting on the 17th.

"The third day, my husband decided he would put me in the ground blind he had been hunting in since opening day," Esther said. "He handed me his muzzleloader, hung up my deer attracting formula and wished me luck. I sat there until noon with no luck. Then I met Doren and we went in for lunch.

"In the afternoon, we returned to the same blinds we had been in during the morning. I wasn't there long before I saw a big doe. She came out of a fencerow then turned around and disappeared into some pine trees.

"Ten minutes later, about 2:00 p.m., I heard something that was about to come out from the same spot the doe did. Figuring it was probably the same deer, I watched and waited. It proved to be the biggest buck I've ever seen. He looked like a tree with legs!

"He was coming straight for the scent my husband put out. I tried to whistle to get the buck to stop for a shot, but I couldn't. Nothing would come out. Then I moved my foot in the leaves to get his attention and that worked."

Esther shot the buck in the neck at a distance of 40 yards. After making the shot, she got up right away to get Doren's attention, so he could help her recover the whitetail. That didn't prove necessary because her husband had seen her shoot the buck. The Frantoms worked out the blood trail together, discovering the deer made it to an irrigation ditch before going down.

"My husband couldn't believe the size of the rack. Later, we found out that the field dressed weight was 200 pounds and the antlers have an inside spread of 23 inches. In February (1999), I won two trophies at the Michigan Deer Spectacular in Lansing for my buck. I was also invited to be on the Michigan Out-of-Doors and Rob Trott's Great Lakes Outdoors TV Programs for their Big Buck Nights."

The three or four-year-old whitetail had an estimated live weight of 260 pounds. The right beam was 24 5/8 inches long and the left antler measured 25 7/8 inches. The rack's second tines were the longest, taping 11 1/8 inches on the right side and 10 5/8 on the left.

Due to webbing of both antlers between the third and fourth tines, the circumference measurements at those points were greater than the bases. The antler bases were 4 2/8 and 4 3/8 inches in circumference. The third circumference on the right side was 4 7/8 and a whopping 7 1/8 inches on the left. Any hunter would be happy with a buck like that. Besides being the state record muzzleloader kill among women, Frantom's buck ranks as the second highest scoring typical on record for women hunting with all types of weapons.

The highest scoring typical buck bagged by a woman in Michigan, according to CBM, is a 12-pointer tagged by Dolores Kassuba from Willis during the 1995 firearms hunt. She got it with a shotgun. The Livingston County whitetail measured 174 1/8. Kassuba outdid all of the men that season. Her buck had the highest scoring typical rack entered in state records for the year.

One of the chapters in Book 2 of <u>Great Michigan Deer Tales</u> tells the story behind Kassuba's record buck. Two more chapters in that book are devoted to state record bucks bagged by women bowhunters. Linda Luna from Lennon arrowed the highest

Brandon Dirschell with his state record nontypical black powder buck that he shot on the last day of the 1999 muzzleloader season. The 20-point antlers measure 187 4/8. Photo courtesy Brandon Dirschell.

scoring nontypical known taken by a female archer in the state during 1993, a 17-pointer that scored 173 1/8. Cora Fink of Quincy holds the state record among typical bow kills for women with a 10-pointer that measured 156.

Nontypical Record

Twenty-year-old Brandon Dirschell from Coldwater will always remember the last day of the 1999 muzzleloader deer season. That's the day he bagged the state's new record nontypical black powder buck in Branch County. The impressive 20-pointer had a gross nontypical score of 202 3/8, according to state record keeper Commemorative Bucks of Michigan (CBM).

The official net score is 187 4/8, almost two full inches more than the previous long-standing record in that category. The reason for almost 15 inches of deductions between the gross and net scores is the left antler has 12 tines versus eight on the right side. The Dirshcell buck beat a 23-pointer shot in Hillsdale County during 1977 by Robert Gendron. The odd-looking Gendron buck scored 185 5/8 and had one antler growing over its right eye.

Brandon's buck ranked fourth among nontypicals for Branch County at the time it was taken. The three that measure more all exceed the minimum of 195 required for entry in national records maintained by the Boone and Crockett Club. The county's first and third nontypicals were taken with shotguns and the second highest scoring was a bow kill.

Mitch Brock claimed the bow killed nontypical in 1995. The 16-pointer measured 200 3/8. The story behind Brock's buck can be found in Book 2 of Great Michigan Deer Tales. The same year that Brock bagged his trophy buck with bow and arrow, Roger Green II bagged a 12-point nontypical in the county that scored 199 7/8. Eric Cain tagged the number one nontypical a year earlier. His 16-pointer measured 201 3/8.

On a statewide basis, more than 100 nontypicals that score more than Dirschell's are listed in CBM records. Most of them were shot with centerfire firearms, but at least nine were collected with bows and arrows. Regardless of how the antlers rank in state records, Brandon is pleased he was able to get the buck that grew such a unique rack. The fact that it's a state record is a bonus.

The buck was his first with a firearm of any kind. Dirschell said he started deer hunting when he was 12 years old with bow and arrow and began trying for whitetails with a gun when he reached the legal age of 14. Brandon had four bucks to his credit with archery equipment when he got the trophy whitetail with a muzzleloader. The biggest of those is a 9-pointer that scores about 110.

"A muzzleloader is the only thing I use during the gun season," he said. "Most of them that are made today are a lot more accurate than shotguns. I shot the buck this year ('99) with a .50 caliber Remington 700. I used to hunt with a Thompson/Center side hammer New Englander. I shot two does with that.

"The farm I killed the record buck on is 1,000 acres in size," Dirschell continued.

"I don't normally have permission to hunt on that farm, but some friends of mine invited me to hunt there with them on the last day of muzzleloader season. They planned on doing some pushes. I don't usually like to participate in drives, but it was a chance to see some new country and perhaps have a chance at a deer, so I decided to go."

There were six hunters in the group. During the first drive of the morning on December 19, 1999, some does were seen, but no shots were taken. It was the second pothole that was pushed where the nontypical was hiding.

Brandon was a stander on that drive. The cover that was to be driven consisted of a grass field that gave way to a 30 acre patch of woods. Dirschell got in a ladder stand that was about 12 feet high in the woodlot. His black powder rifle was loaded with a 280 grain Hornady saboted bullet ahead of two 50 grain Pyrodex pellets.

When the drive started, the buck came out of the grass field and into the woods where Brandon was waiting. A 3x9 power Swift scope was mounted on his front loader. He had the scope on 5 power.

"He was coming right at me when I saw him," Dirschell said. "I wanted to make sure I didn't shoot a small buck. As soon as I saw him, I knew he was a shooter. After that, I didn't look at his rack. I was concentrating on trying to shoot him.

"Because he was coming toward me, I thought I was going to have a close shot, but when he was 90 yards away, he started paralleling me. He was running and I didn't think he was going to stop. I waited for an opening and touched it off.

"My crosshairs were in front of his shoulder when I shot," Brandon remembered. "By the time I shot, the deer had turned angling away. I wasn't sure if I hit him when I shot because of the smoke. The smoke prevented me from seeing any reaction.

"The next time I saw the buck, he was kinda limping, favoring a hind leg. We watched him go all the way across a field and into the woods on the other side. A friend of mine also saw the buck and we talked about how big we thought it was. We thought it was a main frame 8 and maybe a 10, that would be a 130 to 140-inch buck."

Bryan Massey was the friend who also saw the buck on that drive. In fact, Bryan got a shot at the deer, too, after Brandon fired. However, Bryan confirmed that his shot missed. He shot in front of the running buck.

"It was about noon when I shot the buck," Brandon continued. "There was some snow left on the ground from the morning and we were able to find some blood, so we knew I hit the deer. Unsure of where he was hit or how badly he was hurt, we decided to wait an hour and a half before starting to track him.

"Once we started trailing him, we found a lot of blood. He was bleeding a lot. Due to the amount of blood we found, I was hoping we would find him quickly, but he kept going and going.

"The buck eventually crossed onto a farm owned by Stan Banker (Banker was President of CBM at the time). We went to Stan's house to get permission to go after the buck and he allowed us to continue following it. We finally found the buck on Stan's farm. The deer had gone at least three quarters of a mile before going down.

"My bullet hit the deer in the hip and angled forward into the body cavity. The snow that was on the ground was a big help in being able to follow the buck. Without snow, we might not have been able to find him. It took us two and a half to three hours to track the deer to its final resting place.

"When my friend and I actually got up to the buck, we were in shock," Dirschell said. "We couldn't believe he had 20 scorable points. The rack was much bigger than we thought it was."

After Brandon got the buck, Bryan showed him a set of shed antlers he found on a farm adjoining the one where he shot the whitetail that looked similar. The fact that the G3 tine on one beam of the sheds splits and curls downward in the same fashion as the matching tine on the rack worn by the buck, is an indication the sheds are from the same deer. The sheds score in the 160s, with 8 points on one side and 7 on the other. It would not be out of the ordinary for a whitetail that has genetics favoring antler growth to make a substantial increase from one year to the next.

The 20-pointer that Brandon bagged obviously had what it takes to grow an impressive set of antlers quickly. The deer was aged at 3 1/2 and had a dressed weight of 175 pounds. Knowing the whitetail's antlers netted 187 4/8 at that age, it would not be unusual for the same animal's rack to score in the 160s a year earlier. The buck's first set of antlers were very likely impressive as well.

This story would obviously not have had such a happy ending if Stan Banker had not given Dirschell permission to follow the buck onto Stan's property. Banker did consider not granting permission to look for the whitetail, as he pointed out in a column he wrote about the incident for the January/February/March 2000 issue of Buck Fax. As Stan clearly pointed out in the column, he learned a lesson from what happened that day and I think other hunters can, too, so what he wrote is reprinted below with his permission:

Remember What's Important

Has deer hunting become too competitive? I tend to believe that it has. We compete for hunting space, leases, argue over bait piles and shoot small bucks that maybe should be allowed to walk because of the "if I don't the other guy will" mentality. Some hunters may even be tempted to cut corners in order to get that trophy buck so the other guy doesn't.

Competition and jealousy can create an atmosphere that takes away the enjoyment for everyone. These feelings can turn a person into someone that they would never be otherwise. I'm going to relate an incident that I became involved with in the hope that a lesson can be learned.

On December 19th, the last day of the 1999 black powder season, my entire family and I were just sitting down to dinner when we noticed three hunters approaching our backyard from across the property adjoining ours and we correctly guessed that they were going to ask for permission to look for a wounded deer.

My history with the so-called "caretaker" of that property is best described as contentious (we don't get along at all), so my family advised that I deny them access. In the back of my mind, I know that they are right because I believe that if the roles were reversed that I wouldn't receive the same consideration.

But since they did the right thing and came to ask and the fact that they were all very polite young men and the "caretaker" was not among them, I convinced myself to let them go, much to the displeasure of my family.

The hunters told me that one of them had wounded an 8-point buck in about the 120-inch class. After giving them permission to look for the deer, I told them I wanted to see it, if they found it. My primary interest in seeing the buck was to verify for myself that it indeed was shot with a muzzleloader.

They found the whitetail right away about 50 yards from where I had been sitting earlier that morning. Then the rest of their hunting party arrived and asked if they could drive back to get the deer. I was getting angry and told them that they were really pressing their luck with me. But since I wanted to see the buck, I opened some gates and let them go.

They soon came back and I met them at the gate to look at the buck. My attitude slipped several more notches when I saw what was supposed to be an 8-point buck turned into a 20-point nontypical. I was satisfied that it had been shot with a muzzleloader, so with a few more unkind words, I sent them on their way.

The following day, I left on a long trip to southern Indiana, which gave me a long time to think about what had happened. At first, I was angry all over again. Then, the more I thought about it, I wondered why. What had that lucky young man done that was so wrong? Not a thing as far as I could see.

Was it jealousy on my part? Probably a little, but why should I be jealous? I already have three bucks in the book and this will be his first. Any other time, I would be excited for the guy. Why not now? <u>It may be because sometimes competition and jealousy can override common sense.</u>

Had I taken the time to ask a few questions, as I normally would, I would have found out that he wounded the buck about a mile from my place and stuck with the blood trail until he found it. They all should have been commended for the way they handled it. Not treated as they were.

I tried to make it up to the guy by apologizing and seeing to it that he and his buck get the recognition that they deserve. My hope is that you may find a lesson in this incident that you will be able to use sometime. <u>I will file it away in my book of memories, a book more important than any record book.</u>

What Stan wrote in this well done, thought-provoking piece, can also be applied to another trophy whitetail bagged during recent years that is covered in this book - the Rompola buck!

Branch County Muzzleloader Records

This is the former nontypical muzzleloader record whitetail for Michigan. Robert Gendron shot the odd looking 23-pointer in Hillsdale County during 1977. The antlers scored 185 5/8.

Dick Datema (right) and his son Pete with the trophy buck they got during hunt on which they were planning on filling an antlerless permit. The 11-pointer was the highest scoring typical shot in Michigan during 1999, scoring 179 4/8. Photo courtesy Dick Datema.

Chapter 4

Father/Son Trophy

Imagine going deer hunting with the intent of filling an antlerless permit and coming home with a buck that has the highest scoring typical antlers known taken in the entire state for the year. That's what Dick Datema from Haslett and his 12-year-old son Pete did during the fall of 1999 on November 21. The hunt was a chance for father and son to spend time together and for Pete to gain some experience for when he's old enough to hunt whitetails with a firearm himself.

They got far more than they expected. The memory of the hunt on which Datema bagged the impressive 11-pointer will be something they share for the rest of their lives. The antlers have an official net score of 179 4/8, according to state record keeper Commemorative Bucks of Michigan (CBM), easily qualifying for a place in national records maintained by the Boone and Crockett Club as well as high ranking in state records.

The minimum for entry of typical gun kills in CBM records is 125 compared to the much higher score of 170 to meet B&C standards.

Besides being Michigan's best typical for 1999, Datema's buck ranks as the highest scoring typical on record for Ingham County. If it hadn't been for a nontypical point measuring 3 7/8 inches long on the antlers of Dick's buck, which was deducted from the final score, the rack would have netted in the 180s, putting the deer among the state's top 10 typicals. Another booner with 10-point antlers was shot in Ingham County on opening day of the 1995 firearms hunt by Floyd Lee of Woodhaven. That rack measured 171 1/8.

Lee was bowhunting during late October of '95 when he first saw the book buck. Unable to collect it with archery equipment, he was in the same woods when gun season opened. The morning was uneventful. When Floyd hadn't seen any deer by 11:30 from his stand, he started sneak hunting, relying on fresh snow that was on the ground to help muffle his foot steps.

As Floyd was pussy-footing along, he saw the big buck walk out of some brush briefly before returning to the cover. The wind was in his favor, so he moved ahead until he saw the buck's tracks and spotted the whitetail standing 40 yards away. A well placed slug dropped the deer in its tracks. The buck had a dressed weight of 200 pounds and was aged at 3 1/2 years old.

Like so many hunters who tag Michigan's biggest bucks, Dick Datema is not a trophy hunter. He likes to shoot a buck when he can, but takes what comes along. If he happens to be in the right place at the right time to take a trophy animal, as he was during 1999, that's terrific. He's just as happy about taking a monster buck as anyone else would be.

"You can't beat luck when it comes to deer hunting," Datema said. "But, if you hunt a lot, that increases the odds in your favor."

Dick said he's been hunting whitetails in Michigan for about 30 years, having started in 1970. His father owns a camp in the U.P. near Seney and that's where he began his deer hunting career. In fact, he still spends the majority of his deer hunting time at that camp. There's a lot of tradition and memories associated with the family deer camp. The big woods and lack of hunting pressure in that area also appeals to him.

Datema's best U.P. buck is a 7-pointer that was 6 1/2 years old, which he shot during 1980 or '81. Although that buck's antlers are small in comparison to the one he got in '99, it's still a trophy to him, as it should be. Not many bucks reach the age of that one and not all older bucks grow antlers of record book proportions either.

A perfect example of an older U.P. buck that did not grow antlers large enough to qualify for state records is covered in another chapter in this book titled "A Buck Named Lucky."

There was a lot of snow on the ground when Datema got that U.P. 7-pointer. He was sneak hunting along a ridge about 11:00 a.m. when the whitetail came walking into view. Dick said the deer only weighed about 140 pounds.

Datema spent the first days of the '99 firearms season hunting out of the U.P. camp. He shot a forkhorn there on November 17 while hunting with a .308 caliber rifle. One of the biggest bucks that Dick tagged prior to last fall was an 8-pointer he shot in Kent County as a boy. The antlers grown by that whitetail had a 20-inch spread.

He was hunting with a pair of friends he went to school with when he got the 8-pointer. He was lucky enough to be posted on a drive during which the buck and a pair of does came out by him.

Datema said he's an avid duck and pheasant hunter. He usually scouts for the upcoming deer season while bird and waterfowl hunting. The property where Dick got the booner is an abandoned farm with overgrown fields, swales and woodlots. He had seen a lot of deer sign on the parcel, but nothing to indicate a big buck was around.

A friend by the name of Cam Haskins had been bowhunting in the area from a

Father/Son Trophy

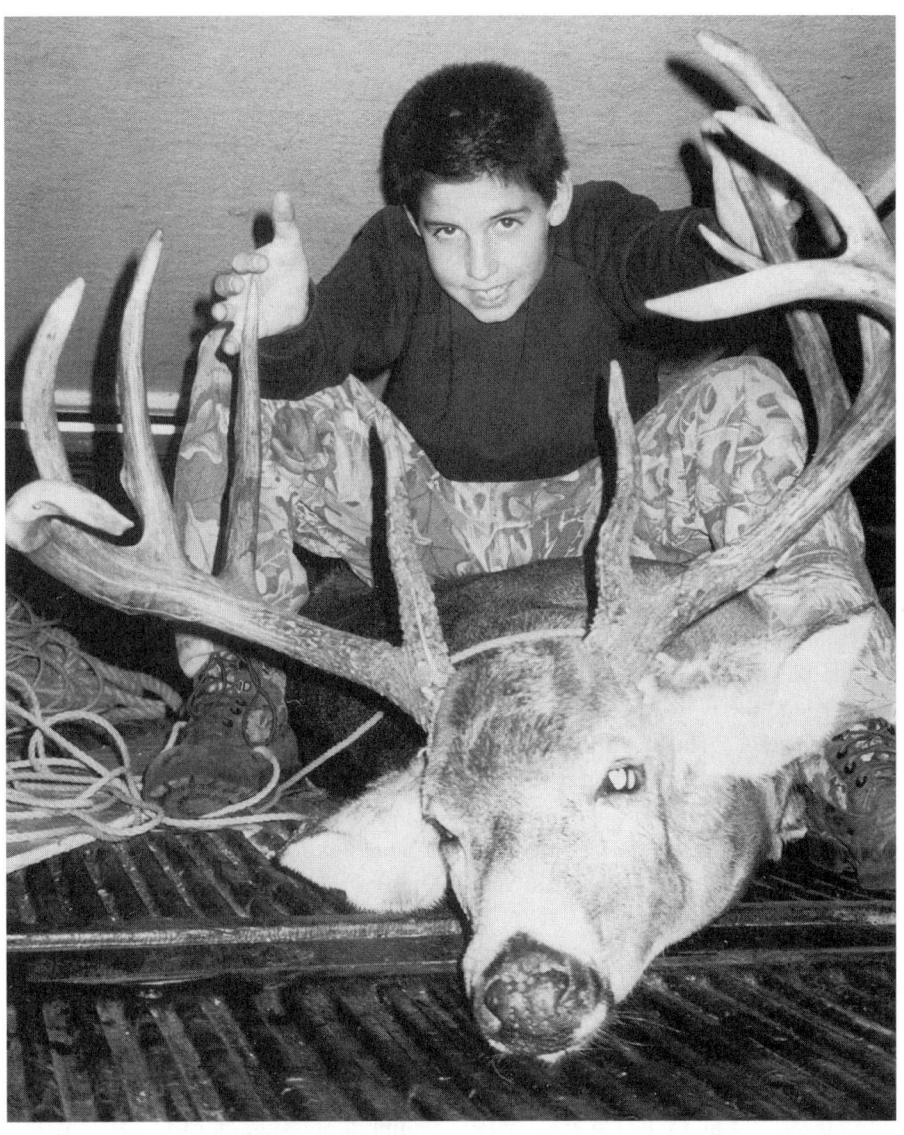

Here's a better view of the Datema buck, with Pete showing the antlers off. The brow tines are exceptionally long, but there's nothing wrong with the other tines either. Photo courtesy Dick Datema.

brush blind Dick helped him prepare and he had seen a big buck. Haskins also saw a trophy whitetail on opening day of gun season. He was hunting with a muzzleloader and took a shot at a small buck. After the shot, he was almost run over by a much bigger whitetail. He told Dick the antlers were at least 20 inches across.

Datema told me that a pair of trophy bucks that were close to the size of the one he got were killed by vehicles on roads in the vicinity. One had 11-point antlers and the other was a 12-pointer. He added that some 40 to 80-acre tracts of land where nobody hunts, serve as refuges for bucks.

On the evening of November 21, Dick and Pete went to a ground blind made of brush in a woodlot that they had not hunted from previously. The sides of the blind were about five feet high, making them tall enough to be above head level when seated. Dick left holes in the sides to be able to shoot through.

Due to the abundance of deer on the property, their intent was to shoot a doe. At 4:50 p.m., they heard a shot from an adjoining farm where a friend of Dick's was hunting. He later found out his buddy got a 6-pointer.

It was 10 minutes after they heard the shot that the father and son saw action. They were only in the blind a little over an hour when Pete spotted a whitetail about 150 yards away.

"There's a deer coming from the right," Pete said.

"I saw it was a buck," Dick commented, "but I couldn't tell how big the antlers were. All I could see were the bases of antlers on top of his head. We watched it walk for 50 yards or more in mature woods. When he reached an eight or nine-foot opening, I shot and he dropped right there."

Dick shot the whitetail with a 12 gauge Remington Model 870 pump shotgun and Remington slugs. The slug took the buck through the shoulders at a distance of about 80 yards. When father and son reached the fallen buck, they were in for a big surprise.

Dick said he thought he shot a small whitetail. He found out that was not the case. The pair were impressed with the size of the deer's antlers.

"Son-of-a-gun, this is a beautiful deer," Dick commented as he looked at the fallen trophy.

Pete said his father walked around the buck for 10 minutes, staring at it and admiring it. Although Dick was impressed with the buck, he didn't really know how big it was by state standards. He might not have had the antlers measured, if it hadn't been for a twist of fate.

Dick's wife Donna works at the DNR office in Lansing. One day she showed wildlife biologist and CBM measurer Pete Squibb a photograph of son Pete with the deer. Squibb said the boy was holding onto the buck's brow tines and there was a lot of antler visible above and below the boy's hands. She also told the scorer that one of the tines was at least a foot long.

The biologist encouraged Donna to bring the antlers in, so he could measure them and she finally did. After measuring the rack, Squibb said he came up with a gross score of 190. Datema had the antlers officially measured at the Michigan Deer Spectacular during February, where he won an award for the best typical for 1999.

Inspite of the large antlers, the buck was not very old. Dick said it was thought to be 2 1/2 or 3 1/2 years old. It was one of those southern Michigan super bucks with phenomenal antler development. The whitetail had a dressed weight of 178 pounds.

The antlers from this impressive buck might not have been measured if Dick's wife Donna, shown here with Pete and the buck, had not taken a photo of the deer to work where it was seen by CBM measurer Pete Squibb.
Photo courtesy Dick Datema.

14-year-old Craig Rodosalewicz with his first deer, a Boone and Crockett nontypical. Craig's mother saw the buck a number of times before deer season opened. Photo courtesy Craig Rodosalewicz.

Chapter 5

A Happy 14-year-old

The next time Jackie Rodosalewicz from Tecumseh tells her husband Steve that she's seen a buck with a monster rack, he will be more likely to believe her description of the rack's dimensions. When she told him about such a sighting on their Lenawee County property during 1998, he doubted that she saw a whitetail with antlers as big as she claimed they were. He thought she was exaggerating.

It took their 14-year-old son Craig to prove his mother right. He shot the record book whitetail on the morning of November 16 during his first hour of deer hunting with a firearm. The deer's huge nontypical rack has 14 points that had a final official net score of 195, according to Commemorative Bucks of Michigan (CBM).

That score equals the minimum necessary for entry of nontypical antlers in national records maintained by the Boone and Crockett Club, an achievement that has many veteran hunters envious of Craig's success. The antlers were the second highest scoring nontypicals known taken with firearms in Michigan during 1998 seasons. The county has produced a number of other booners over the years, both typicals and nontypicals, making Lenawee one of the better counties in the state for big racks.

The county's number one nontypical was taken by a bowhunter. Paul Kintner from Adrian collected a 19-pointer in Lenawee County during 1996 that scored 211. The story behind Kintner's trophy bow kill can be found in Book 2 of <u>Great Michigan Deer Tales</u>.

The other pair of B&C nontypicals listed for the county in state records besides Craig's, when this was written, were also bagged with shotguns. Fred Hood, Jr. of Ottawa Lake tagged the larger of the two, an 18-pointer that measured 202 2/8. He got the buck that grew the record book rack on opening morning of the 1988 firearms season.

Hood used a brushpile as a natural blind that gave him a good view of surrounding fields and a pair of lanes that bucks had been using that merged 50 yards away. The huge nontypical stepped into a winter wheat field at first light long enough for Fred to connect with his shotgun. A local farmer later sent Hood a video that he had taken of the trophy buck from his combine before deer season opened.

The county's highest scoring typical, according to CBM, is a 13-pointer that Oscar Lopez from Adrian got during 1991 that measured 174 4/8. That whitetail was the first one Lopez ever shot and he did it with a borrowed shotgun. He connected on opening day of gun season about 9:00 a.m.

Oscar said he was walking toward his son in a large field with high grass when he jumped the buck and a doe. He fired a slug from the 12 gauge shotgun first, followed by a load of buckshot and the buckshot connected. The buck was aged at 6 1/2 and dressed out at 201 pounds.

The Rodosalewiczs are a deer hunting family. Steve had been hunting whitetails for 28 years by 1998 and Jackie wasn't far behind with 25 years of experience. They are also a two season family, enjoying bowhunting as well as trying their luck with firearms.

It was only natural that Craig followed his parents' examples. He started bowhunting for whitetails at the age of 12. The boy took a shot at a doe from a tree stand during the fall of 1997, but his arrow missed, hitting right under the whitetail.

Craig enjoyed even more excitement on opening day of the 1998 bow season.

"Two bucks were having a pretty good fight in front of me 70 to 80 yards away. One was a 4-point and the other was a 6-point. They were too far away for a shot with my bow, but I wish I would have had a camera with me. I would have shot them with that.

"They were really clanging their antlers together. The fight lasted about three minutes."

Jackie saw the monster nontypical that her son eventually shot, on a number of occasions during 1998, starting in the summer when local bucks were in a bachelor group. She got her best look at the whitetail during bow season, but she wasn't hunting at the time. The family raises Morgan horses on their property and Jackie was leading horses out to the pasture from the barn.

While leading one of the horses, the huge nontypical walked by 75 feet away, apparently unconcerned about the presence of the human. The buck was used to being around the horses. That sighting took place between 9:00 and 9:30 a.m. Jackie was obviously impressed by the buck's antlers, but she couldn't get her husband to believe how big they really were.

Jackie also saw the booner on the evening of November 15th about 5:00 p.m. as it trotted through their pasture. If it weren't for the no Sunday hunting regulation in Lenawee County, Jackie herself might have killed the monster whitetail. Due to the restriction on Sunday hunting, the Rodosalewiczs had to wait until Monday to begin deer hunting with shotguns on their property.

Craig said his father talked him into hunting from a blind (hut) behind the barn in

A Happy 14-year-old

an open hayfield for his first attempt at a whitetail with a shotgun. The boy said he was looking forward to hunting with a gun because he saw it as a chance for him to finally get a deer. He was looking forward to filling a tag with a whitetail of either sex. It didn't matter to him whether it was a buck or doe.

The beginning hunter was in position before daylight. His first wildlife encounter of the morning was with a mouse rather than a deer.

"A mouse lives in the hut where I was hunting and his movements were bugging me. It finally got in one of the windows and I knocked it out.

After that I was sitting back not expecting to see anything when I decided to get a deer call I brought with me.

"Everytime I reach down to get the call, a deer shows up. It's happened every year. I don't understand why. It's some kind of phenomenon.

"I bent over and unzipped the pouch where the call was. Before I took the call out, I looked back up and there he was just standing there. He jumped the fence and started coming toward me.

"I put the shotgun barrel out one of the windows and started following him, so I would be ready to shoot when he got close enough. The way he was coming, I had to switch windows so I could keep following him. In the process, I knocked my chair over and it fell on the floor.

"I thought the noise might spook the buck, but it didn't bother the deer. He just kept trotting, looking at the barn. When he was about 70 yards away, I shot and he dropped right there."

Craig was shooting a 12 gauge Remington 870 with Remington rifled slugs. The slug struck the whitetail at the base of the neck, breaking it and killing the whitetail instantly. As soon as the buck was down, Craig grabbed a walkie talkie his parents had given him, so they could communicate with him. He was anxious to tell them he got his first whitetail.

In his excitement, Craig was talking too fast for them to understand what he was saying. After they got him to calm down somewhat and talk more slowly, here's how the conversation went:

"Dad, he's dead!"

"What do you mean he," Steve questioned, figuring his son had shot a doe.

"It's a buck!"

"Is it a spike?"

"No. It's much bigger than that," Craig responded.

"How many points?"

It took Craig a while to answer that question because he had to leave the hut and walk up to the buck to count the tines.

"It's got 13 points!"

Craig was obviously still excited and he missed one of the points during his count. His parents thought the count might be on the high side instead of low, so Jackie decided to investigate. It didn't take her long to realize the buck was the one she had been seeing and she came up with an accurate count of points. She then managed to talk Steve into coming for a look.

Craig and Jackie were standing side-by-side to block Steve's view of the whitetail as he approached. They did that intentionally so they could watch his reaction when he saw the size of the antlers. As expected, his jaw dropped when they stepped aside. There was no way he could question the size of the buck Jackie had been seeing any longer.

The trophy buck was aged at 4 1/2 and had a dressed weight of 200 pounds. It was 7:45 a.m. when Craig shot the deer. As it turns out, Steve and Craig had found one of the buck's shed antlers during 1997 that it would have grown the previous year. The deer would have had a 10-point rack at the time.

Family friend John Hoeft was hunting with the Rodosalewiczs the morning that Craig got the big buck. Hoeft also scored that morning, shooting a 5-pointer with an unbalanced rack.

Craig's whitetail hunting education continued the following Saturday when he hunted during the afternoon with his mother. A trio of does came within range of his shotgun while hunting from a different spot and he got two of them. The boy did a super job of supplying the family with venison during '98. Neither Steve or Jackie ended up filling a tag.

Craig with his first whitetail where he dropped it with a slug on November 16, 1998. Photo courtesy Craig Rodosalewicz.

A Happy 14-year-old

Craig's father Steve congratulates him for bagging a trophy buck that Craig's mother saw on a number of occasions before the boy got it.
Photo courtesy Craig Rodosalewicz.

Chuck Goodfellow with the booner he bagged in Sanilac County on the morning of November 15, 1998 after shooting a 5-point. The nontypical antlers have 20 points and score 197 2/8. Photo courtesy Chuck Goodfellow.

Chapter 6

Thumbs Up Booners

A pair of Boone and Crockett class bucks were bagged from counties in the thumb during the 1998 firearms season. One was a nontypical and the other was a typical. Chuck Goodfellow from Marlette bagged the nontypical in Sanilac County and James Hurd from Capac got the typical. Read on for the stories behind both successful hunts.

The Goodfellow Buck

Chuck Goodfellow from Marlette bagged the first booner know taken in Sanilac County, according to state records maintained by Commemorative Bucks of Michigan (CBM). He scored on the world class whitetail on opening morning of the 1998 firearms season.

It was a 20-point nontypical scoring 197 2/8. A minimum score of 195 is necessary for nontypical antlers to qualify for a place in national records compiled by Boone and Crockett. To be considered for state records, nontypical racks must measure at least 150.

The 20-pointer that Goodfellow tagged that fall was not only the first gun kill from the county to qualify for national records, it is the highest scoring nontypical known taken by a gun hunter in the state for 1998, according to CBM. Another B&C nontypical was shot by 14-year-old Craig Rodosalewicz from Tecumseh in Lenawee County on November 16. That 14-pointer measured 195 on the nose. Another chapter in this book is devoted to the Rodosalewicz buck.

Although Chuck collected the number one gun kill for '98, in terms of antler score, 20-year-old Donnie Bollinger from Gregory got another world class nontypical in Washtenaw County with bow and arrow on October 9 that was larger. He got a 22-pointer that measured 200 1/8. A chapter about that buck can be found elsewhere in this book.

The number one nontypical on record for Sanilac County prior to '98 was a 16-pointer that Donald Smelser shot during 1996. That rack measured 190 3/8.

Although no B&C bucks had previously been recorded for Sanilac County, world class nontypicals had been documented in the adjoining counties of Huron and Tuscola. Perhaps some of the same genetics spilled over into Sanilac. Patrick Flanagan, Jr. scored on a big 24-pointer in Huron County during 1990 that measured 215 5/8. One of the chapters in Book 1 of <u>Great Michigan Deer Tales</u> is devoted to the story behind that buck. A pair of nontypicals scoring 205 1/8 and 211 3/8 were shot in Tuscola County, but they were tagged during 1951 and 1948 respectively.

From Goodfellow's perspective prior to November 15, 1998, he wondered if he would ever shoot a buck with antlers large enough to have the head mounted. He figured a rack should be 10 points or better before the head would be mountable, unless it was an exceptional 8-point. His best buck out of the 19 or 20 he got prior to '98 was an 8-pointer he tagged during 1993, but he didn't consider those antlers large enough for a mount.

Chuck said he had seen three or four nice bucks that he considered mountable during his 33 years of whitetail hunting, but he was usually bowhunting when he saw them and they were never in position for a bow shot. He watched one of those trophy class bucks that he thought he had his best chance at, during 1984 and '85. The buck had 10 points in '84 and the deer grew 12-point antlers during '85.

Unfortunately, a neighbor shot the whitetail before Chuck could. Goodfellow said his neighbor didn't have the antlers measured, but he guessed they would score in the 140s.

Chuck said he thinks he saw the big buck he got during 1998 on two occasions prior to shooting it. He got a glimpse of it once when coming home. It was gone before he was able to get binoculars on it, but the large rack on its head was obvious.

He also saw the whitetail on opening day of the 1997 firearms season. His neighbor had killed a buck soon after daylight that year, so Chuck offered to haul it out of the woods on his 4-wheeler. Goodfellow was in the process of getting his ATV when he saw the big buck on the edge of the woods about 150 yards away. It was gone again before he could get a good look at the rack, but he knew it had to be at least a 10-pointer.

Opening morning of the 1998 firearms season found Chuck posted within 20 yards of where he had seen the trophy whitetail the year before.

He was sitting with his trusty 20 gauge Ithaca Deerslayer shotgun that he had relied on to collect venison for 15 to 20 years. The gun was mounted with a 4 power Leupold scope and it was loaded with 2 3/4-inch Brenneke slugs.

"I really like Brennekes," Goodfellow said. "They're accurate and I've never lost a deer with them. I don't want to wound a deer, so I always make sure I've got a good shot before I take it. If I'm unsure of making a killing shot, I don't shoot. I'd rather let one go than wound it."

It started raining lightly right at daylight, but Chuck didn't have to wait long for action.

"I shot a 5-point at 7:20. He was 65 yards away broadside when I shot him. I watched him run 30 yards and drop on the edge of the woods. I decided to have a cup of coffee before going over to the deer," the veteran hunter commented.

That decision reflects Chuck's experience as a deer hunter. He was laid back enough to relax and allow himself the luxury of a cup of coffee now that he knew one of his buck tags was filled. He was confident the buck was dead and there was no rush to field dress it. The long time hunter could savor the feeling of success at the same time he enjoyed the warmth and taste of the coffee.

Taking the time out for coffee also played a critical role in Chuck collecting one of Michigan's best bucks for 1998. If he had gone to the fallen 5-pointer right away, like many novices would have been inclined to, he might not have gotten the trophy nontypical. Barely five or six minutes went by after the young buck was down when Goodfellow heard a shot behind him not far away.

He instinctively turned to look in that direction and he saw a sight he will never forget. The shot had spooked the trophy buck and a pair of other deer. They were running in Chuck's direction, with the buck leading the way.

The whitetail's big rack was obvious. He knew it was at least a 10 point and he got ready to shoot. When it was 60 yards away and broadside, Goodfellow put the crosshairs on its shoulder and fired.

"He dropped when I shot," Chuck said. "Then he started to get back up and I shot again. I didn't want to lose this guy."

His first shot broke the buck's back. He aimed for the neck with his second round and that slug killed the deer. Although the neck shot had the desired effect, he realized later that he probably should have put the finishing shot behind the buck's shoulder rather than through the neck. The exit wound made a big hole in the cape that the taxidermist had a difficult time repairing.

There was no doubt in Chuck's mind that he had a mountable buck after getting that one. At the time he got it though, putting it down was the first thing on his mind.

"I knew it was a good one when I walked up to it," Goodfellow said, "but I didn't realize he was as big as he is. I was just happy to get it. I didn't expect anything like this."

Chuck was hunting with Dennis Smith. It was Smith who shot and spooked the book buck into his neighbor. Dennis had taken a doe.

"When I got to the buck, I counted 15 or 16 points," Chuck said. "That's what I told Dennis when he got there. After he counted the points he said, 'You better count them again. I counted 21.'"

The rack does have 21 projections, but one of them is less than an inch in length. For official scoring purposes, tines have to be at least an inch long to be considered.

"I wouldn't have had this one scored if it wasn't for my wife," Chuck commented.

James Hurd with his St. Clair County trophy. The 13-point typical scores 171. The hunter saw the buck while bowhunting three years in a row before finally getting it with a shotgun. Photo courtesy James Hurd.

"She was on the telephone making the arrangements soon after I got it. It didn't take long for word to spread about the buck. We had over 130 people stop by our house to see the deer in just two days."

The antlers have five-inch bases and beams that are about 27 inches long. There are nine points on one side and 11 on the other. Chuck said the rack has a typical 10-point frame with a lot of shorter nontypical points that he couldn't see when the whitetail was running toward him.

The buck was 4 1/2 years old and had a dressed weight of 250 pounds. Its neck measured 27 3/4 inches around. Chuck said he shot an older buck about five years earlier. It was aged at 6 1/2 and weighed 217 pounds. The 7-point antlers that buck grew weren't anything exceptional.

Regardless of how Goodfellow's buck ranks in state and national records, it's his personal best and that's all that counts for him. The 1998 firearms season will also go down as one of the best in his personal records. He had more action over a shorter period of time than ever before. He hunted less than an hour and filled both of his buck tags, putting one of them on the biggest buck he's ever seen, not to mention most of the other hunters in the state.

The 1994 season was one of Chuck's best until '98. He shot a 6-point at 7:25 opening morning and didn't hunt again until Thanksgiving morning. He got another buck at 7:25 that day, not hunting more than 1 1/2 hours to fill two tags.

The Hurd Buck

One of the highest scoring typical antlered whitetails known taken in the state during 1998 came from the Thumb's St. Clair County. It was a 13-pointer measuring 171 that James Hurd from Capac shot on November 16. Interestingly, that rack scores exactly the same as the county's previous number one typical.

John D. Pierce from Romeo collected an 11-pointer from the county on November 16, 1995 that ended up with an official net score of 171. It's an amazing coincidence that the county's only two Boone and Crockett qualifiers have the exact same score. A minimum score of 170 is required for entry in national records maintained by B&C. Typical gun kills only have to measure 125 to meet the minimum for entry in state records.

The fact that both booners were taken over a span of four years indicates the quality of bucks from the county is increasing. That trend may include other counties in the Thumb, too, because Hurd's buck is the second B&C qualifier entered in state records from '98.

One other county in the Thumb besides St. Clair, Sanilac, Huron and Tuscola - Lapeer - has produced its share of book bucks during recent years, one of which was a B&C nontypical. However that whitetail was a road kill that was found dead during November of 1993. The 26-pointer scored 221 2/8. The county's highest scoring typical measured 174 2/8. Barry Worvie got that 10-point during the 1983 gun season.

Jim Hurd saw the 13-pointer he got during '98 in St. Clair County over a period of three years before finally getting it. Most of his sightings of the buck were while bowhunting. The whitetail was within bow range each time he saw the buck prior to November 16, 1998, but something always prevented him from getting a shot.

The buck actually has 10 typical points and that's what Jim thought it had each time he saw it. He said the tines simply got longer each year. When he finally got the whitetail in 1998, the rack had three short nontypicals points, two of which were on the right antler.

A pair of the sticker points were exactly an inch long, which is the minimum length to be considered a legal point. The third one measured 1 2/8 inches long. None of the nontypical points would have been easy to see under hunting conditions.

"The first time I saw him was three years ago," Hurd commented after getting the whitetail. "That would have been 1996. He was a real nice 10-point then. He came under my tree stand as I started to get down. It was too dark to shoot, but I could clearly see those light colored antlers.

"In 1997 I saw him from the same stand as a blizzard started. He got within 20 or 30 yards of me, but he was downwind. He eventually smelled me and took off before I could get a shot."

Jim had the exceptional buck within five yards of him while bowhunting a couple of days before the 1998 firearms season opened. He was hunting in the same tree stand he had seen the whitetail from the two previous years.

"I was watching a smaller buck and a doe in a wheat field. I had a grunt call with me, so I grunted a few times to try to get the small buck to come closer. The big one came in instead. I think he was bedded nearby.

"He came almost under my stand, but it was real thick and brushy, so I wasn't able to get a shot then either."

As a veteran of more than 20 years of whitetail hunting, Jim knew the buck that was so close to him that day had a much bigger rack than any other deer he had taken previously. He had tagged some nice bucks with both bow and gun in Jackson and Calhoun Counties, but nothing as nice as that. His best bucks up until then were 8-pointers with 17-inch spreads, one of which had 11-inch tines, but he hadn't had the antlers of any of the bucks he bagged previously measured.

To increase his chances of connecting on the trophy whitetail during gun season, Hurd put a tree stand near its bedding area. The location was too thick to hunt with bow and arrow, but a shotgun and slugs would give him the coverage he needed. The tree stand he put up to hunt from with a shotgun gave him a view of the bedding area as well as where he had seen the deer while bowhunting. The platform was 16 to 18 feet from the ground in a tree line along the edge of a small woods.

No Sunday hunting is allowed in St. Clair County and November 15th fell on a Sunday that year, so Jim had to wait until the 16th to find out if his new stand location would pay off. Soon after it was light enough to see on the 16th, Hurd saw some cars stopped on a road that borders a big field the big buck had been feeding in. He thought the vehicles' occupants were looking at deer and he didn't have to wait long to confirm that.

Soon after he noticed the stopped cars, he saw a couple of deer coming across the wheat field toward him. They were too far away at that point to see if either one of them was a buck. But by the time they were 150 yards away, Jim saw antlers and realized one of the deer was the buck he had been seeing while bowhunting. The second whitetail was a doe.

The whitetails started running and the buck was in the lead, but the hunter said he didn't want to risk a running shot at that distance. His patience paid off. When 100 yards away, the booner stopped and looked back at the doe. Hurd was confident in his ability to connect on a stationary target at that distance and took advantage of the opportunity, dropping the buck.

He was shooting 2 3/4-inch Brenneke slugs out of the 12 gauge, smoothbore barrel of his Beretta shotgun. He said he's able to get better groups with that brand of slug out of his smoothbore than with saboted slugs out of rifled slug barrels. He has a two power Tasco scope mounted on his shotgun.

Although Jim got his booner from a tree stand and he took advantage of the new rule that went into effect that year allowing firearms hunters to hunt from elevated platforms, he felt he still would have gotten the buck if he would have been required to hunt from the ground. He said he simply would have selected a different location to try to ambush the buck. He had a spot in mind that still would have put him in position to intercept the whitetail on the morning of November 16.

The whitetail was thought to be 5 1/2 or 6 1/2 years old and dressed out at just over 200 pounds. The booner that John Pierce shot in St. Clair County during '95 was aged at 6 1/2 and had a dressed weight of 218 pounds, so both bucks were similar in other ways besides antler score.

The antlers from Hurd's buck have a 19-inch inside spread, with right and left antlers measuring 25 7/8 and 26 2/8 inches in length respectively. The second tines on both beams were 12 2/8 and 12 6/8 inches long. The third tines were more than 11 inches long on both sides.

Donnie Bollinger is obviously happy about taking this 22-pointer scoring 200 1/8 during a rushed bow hunt in Washtenaw County on the evening of October 9, 1998. Photo courtesy Donnie Bollinger.

Chapter 7

Bollinger's Bow Buck

Most of Michigan's biggest bucks are bagged when it's least expected and the highest scoring nontypical known taken in the state by a bowhunter during the fall of 1998 was no exception. Imagine climbing into a tree stand barely 30 minutes before dark and having a huge buck with a massive, many-tined, Boone and Crockett qualifying rack walk into view 20 minutes later to offer you a gimme shot.

Impossible? Maybe for you and I, but that's what happened for 20-year-old Donnie Bollinger from Gregory on the evening of October 9, 1998 in Washtenaw County.

Bollinger would have been happy to take any buck that evening and was even entertaining the thought of taking a doe because he was anxious to get some meat in the freezer. Instead, he arrowed a 22-pointer that had a net score of 200 1/8. Nontypical antlers have to score a minimum of 195 to qualify for a place in national records maintained by the Boone and Crockett Club and the Bollinger buck easily did that.

Either gun or bow kills that meet the minimums can be listed in B&C records. The Pope and Young Club compiles national bowhunting records and the minimum score for entry of nontypicals in their book is 150. Nontypical bow kills that measure at least 125 qualify for a place in state records handled by Commemorative Bucks of Michigan (CBM).

The antlers from Bollinger's buck will not only be put in state records, they will be near the top of the list of nontypical bow kills in Michigan. When this was written, they were in the number six spot behind a 16-pointer Mitch Brock from Coldwater got in Branch County on the last day of October in 1995 that scores 200 3/8.

The number four nontypical with bow and arrow scoring 203 6/8, also came from Washtenaw County. It was an 18-pointer bagged by Rick Chabot from Ann Arbor on October 31, 1996. That rack is the highest scoring nontypical on record for the county.

The number two nontypical bow kill for the entire state was shot the same day as Chabot's in Lenawee County by Paul Kintner from Adrian. That 19-pointer measured an even 211. The stories behind the Kintner and Chabot bucks are included in the same chapter in Book 2 of Great Michigan Deer Tales.

On the county level, Bollinger's buck presently ranks second among alltime nontypicals for Washtenaw County. This county has produced an exceptional number of booners for both gun and bow hunters, most of which have been typicals.

Although young in years, Donnie Bollinger, is an experienced bowhunter. He started bowhunting at the age of 12, the youngest age possible in Michigan, and he had taken at least one whitetail a year with archery equipment since then. Most years he tagged multiple deer during bow seasons.

He had taken his share of young bucks with spikes, 5 points and 6 points. His best buck with bow and arrow prior to the fall of 1998 was a 7-pointer he shot during 1997. That whitetail had a 16-inch spread.

"I've seen big bucks before," Bollinger said, "but most of them never came close enough for a bow shot."

The lone exception was during the fall of 1996 when Donnie had a shot at a trophy whitetail that he thinks is the same one that he got during 1998. It was December and the late bow season was open. A friend of Bollinger's had seen the big buck the evening before, but it was too far away to try a shot. The next morning, Donnie was in a tree stand where the whitetail had been seen.

"He came out where my buddy saw him the evening before," Bollinger told me. "The buck was 25 yards away and I figured I could get him, but I missed. My arrow went right underneath him.

"It was cold that day and there was a foot and a half of snow on the ground. My hands were numb. I got excited and shot too soon."

Donnie said he thinks the buck's antlers were bigger then than when he finally got the deer. At least they looked bigger. He said the rack had lots of points like it did during '98, but he thinks the beams were wider. It's possible the deer could have been a different one, too.

Bollinger hunts a farm owned by his grandfather. He said a buck like the one he got had been seen on the farm for four years. A B&C buck was the furthest thing from his mind when he climbed into a tree stand on the edge of a field and a swamp on October 9, 1998.

He got off of work later than normal that Friday, and the only thing on his mind when he left work was to try to get into his stand to do some bowhunting as soon as possible. He wanted to get into position quickly to avoid spooking deer that he knew would be starting to feed any time. He changed into his Realtree Advantage camouflage clothes, grabbed his 72-pound pull Clearwater overdraw bow, Tru Flite release and was off.

Donnie was especially confident of his ability with the bow and his Easton XX75

2213 superlight arrows that evening. The night before, he and Ryan Huck from Fowlerville had gone through a four hour practice session in the pole barn to make sure their equipment was on and it was. Bollinger said he enjoys shooting bows and arrows and practices when ever he gets the chance.

Huck had tagged a forkhorn on the first evening of bow season and Bollinger was anxious to punch one of his tags. He had seen a lot of deer while bowhunting since the season began, but none had presented him with a good bow shot. He figured it was just a matter of time before he got a shot and he was obviously right.

The archer was relieved when no deer were in sight as he approached the same tree stand where his buddy had scored. The stand, which was placed in an oak tree, actually belonged to Donnie's younger brother Jake. Jake didn't mind his brother hunting from the spot.

Donnie quickly climbed the 20 feet to reach his brother's Loc-on Stand and relaxed once in place, hoping deer would soon arrive, and they did. He was only in his perch about 10 minutes when a doe appeared and moved into the field to feed. She was soon followed by a steady stream of other antlerless deer. There were 13 or 14 does and fawns feeding to Donnie's left when he noticed all of them were looking at something along the edge of the woods to his right. Light was fading fast at that point.

When the bowhunter followed their gaze, he was thrilled to see a buck of a lifetime. He was elated when the big deer walked right toward his stand. However, when it was 15 yards away, the trophy whitetail stopped and looked right up at him. At least he thought it was looking at him.

Donnie held his breath, fearing the buck was going to see him and bolt. The deer didn't see anything that alerted it though and soon put its head down, stepping closer to some apples Bollinger had put out 12 yards away. When the whitetail moved into a good position for a shot, Donnie was ready. He sent a 90 grain Rocky Mountain broadhead through its chest cavity.

The buck didn't go far. It only made it 40 yards into the field before piling up. Donnie's eyes were glued to the animal's every move and his excitement came gushing out when the whitetail went down.

Donnie said he thought the buck was a big 10 or 12-pointer at the time he shot it. When he reached the fallen buck, he tried to count the antler points and came up with 20. He couldn't wait any longer to share his excitement after counting antler tines. He ran to his truck and called friends and family on his cell phone to give them the news.

When his father arrived, he asked how many points the rack had and Donnie told him 20. The elder Bollinger didn't waste any time double checking the points and when he finished he said, "I think there's 22 scorable points." He proved to be right.

What did Donnie's younger brother think about him taking such a big buck from his stand?

"He deserved it," Jake said. "He's been hunting a long time."

One interesting feature about the antlers from Bollinger's buck, besides their size, is a hollow "bubble" on the left beam. The antler cavity was probably created by a parasite when the rack was in velvet. Botflies commonly lay eggs in developing antlers and the larvae frequently leave holes in the bone when they transform into adults and fly away. The cavity on this particular rack is larger than normal and so was everything else.

"When that buck came in, he acted like he was King," Bollinger said. The deer probably was King of that area. The once-in-a-lifetime buck had a dressed weight of 215 pounds. It was 5 1/2 or 6 1/2 years old. Jim and Sons Taxidermy from Chelsea mounted the buck's head for Donnie and he is pleased with the job they did.

The big nontypical is not the only good buck Donnie bagged during '98. On opening day of firearms season he shot his second best buck ever, a 9-pointer. That ended his hunting for the year.

Donnie with his impressive bow-bagged buck that dressed out at 215 pounds. Photo courtesy Donnie Bollinger.

The left beam of the Bollinger buck has a large hollow bubble on the outside that's visible in this photo of the hanging head mount.

Rick Hanson with Michigan's highest scoring typical from 1997. The 10-pointer scored 188 1/8, putting it near the top of the state's records. Photo courtesy Rick Hanson.

Chapter 8

Michigan's Hanson Buck

Deer hunters with the last name of Hanson may have a knack for bagging world class bucks. Milo Hanson from Biggar, Saskatchewan tagged the world record typical whitetail near his home during the fall of 1993. Rick Hanson from Napoleon, Michigan tagged one of his home state's biggest typicals in Jackson County.

It's no secret that Jackson County produces some of the biggest antlered whitetails in Michigan. That county has given up the highest scoring typicals known taken in the state a number of years. One of those years was 1997. That was the year that Rick Hanson took state honors for the highest scoring typical with a huge 10-pointer that measured 188 1/8.

The year before, Troy Stephens from Jackson bagged a new state record typical in the same county. The 16-pointer scored 198. If you want to read about how Troy got his buck and see some photographs of it, refer to Book 2 of <u>Great Michigan Deer Tales</u>.

Even though the Stephens deer has almost 10 inches more antler than Hanson's, the "smaller" rack is still far bigger than most deer hunters will ever see. Its dimensions easily qualify it for a spot in state and national records. Typical gun kills must measure a minimum of 125 to qualify for state records, but it requires at least 170 inches of antler to make it into national records maintained by the Boone and Crockett Club. Rick's rack surpasses that by more than 18 inches.

Although the antlers from Hanson's buck don't come close to challenging the Stephens' deer, they still rank way up there in alltime records maintained by Commemorative Bucks of Michigan (CBM). They rank second among gun kills. A typical bow kill from Jackson County also scores more than the Hanson head. Craig Calderone arrowed that whitetail during 1986. That 14-pointer has an official score of 193 2/8.

You won't find Calderone's buck listed in state records, but it is listed in records maintained by the Boone and Crockett and Pope and Young Clubs. To read the story behind the Calderone buck and to find out why it's not in CBM records, refer to a chapter in Book 1 of Great Michigan Deer Tales.

The spot where Hanson connected on his Boone and Crockett buck has been good to him. The booner was the fifth buck he's shot there in as many years. The other four whitetails were much smaller. The biggest of those four was an 8-pointer he tagged during 1996. Coincidentally, he got that buck on the same date and time as the book deer.

It was at 8:00 a.m. on November 16, 1996 when Rick got the 8-point. There was a cut cornfield in front of where he was sitting. He watched the buck walk across the cut corn until it stopped 30 yards away and looked back the way it came from.

Hanson took advantage of that opportunity to send a Remington rifled slug from his Remington Model 1100 12 gauge on a collison course with the buck's shoulder. The whitetail never knew what hit him, collapsing on the spot.

Rick said he saw a lot of bucks near his home during 1996, including the 8-point he eventually shot. "One day during bow season I saw seven different bucks in a field when I came home," he said. "I saw the 8-point quite a bit. He was a young buck that weighed around 150 pounds.

"A pair of 10-points that I couldn't tell apart were among the bucks I saw during 1996," Hanson continued. "Maybe one of them was the one I shot during 1997. All of the land where I live is private, so hunting pressure is light. There's thick cover in the area and lots of corn, giving the bucks plenty of places to hide."

The three bucks Rick shot from his hot spot prior to the 8-pointer were yearlings with 3, 4 and 5-point antlers. Those bucks were all shot during the afternoon. The fact that the location where Hanson has met with consistent success is within view of his home enabled his wife to observe routine deer activity there. She urged him to hunt there and he's glad he paid attention to her.

"I used to hunt further back in the woods away from the house," Rick said. "I would frequently come home without seeing anything and my wife would tell me about seeing deer closer to the house. I saw the same thing happen one time when a neighbor walked back to where I used to hunt."

The terrain in the area funnels whitetails through the spot he watches during gun season. That's why it's so productive. The fact that he saw and missed a nice buck from the furthest location made it harder for him to move to the closer spot, but once he did, he's hunted there ever since.

It was the abundance of deer in the area where Rick lives that served as an incentive for him to take up deer hunting in the first place. He said he didn't hunt until he moved to that location. Some of his neighbors hunted and they got him interested in trying it.

He started deer hunting 18 years before he got the exceptional whitetail. He hunted for three years before getting his first deer, a 9-pointer. He's been hooked ever since.

Even though Rick hadn't been successful in taking a big buck himself prior to

1997, he knew there were some in the vicinity besides the one he missed. He saw trophy 12 and 13-point bucks taken on adjoining property during 1993 and '94. Then he saw the pair of 10-points during 1996.

Rick said he didn't see many bucks nearby during 1997 and he was wondering if any were around. Buck sign normally starts appearing during bow season, but he didn't see any rubs and scrapes that November until two or three days before firearm season opened. The sign he saw just before gun season confirmed that at least one buck was in the area, but he didn't have any idea how big the deer was. He certainly didn't expect to see anything as big as the whitetail he got.

After an uneventful opening day, Hanson was back in position at his favorite funnel the morning of November 16. He was sitting on a stool in the open. The cornfield in front of him was not cut, but the booner came from behind him. It's a good thing the book buck was preoccupied with the scent of a doe that probably went through the area before daylight because if the deer had been alert, it would have seen Rick and probably left without him ever knowing it had been there.

As luck would have it, the exceptional whitetail came around to Hanson's right side with its nose to the ground. The deer was only 20 yards away when Rick saw it. The distance between the two was about half that by the time the hunter reacted by raising his shotgun. The buck saw the movement right away and turned to go back where he came from.

"I have a low power Bushnell scope on my shotgun, but it didn't do me any good," Rick said. "I never got him in the scope. I just pulled up and shot. I'm not sure if the gun got to my shoulder or not."

What ever Hanson did as far as shooting, it worked. The fact that the buck was so close worked to his advantage. Rick got off three shots, the first two of which connected. However, the first slug only grazed the top of the back.

The whitetail went down after the second shot, but quickly jumped back up and took off. That's when Rick shot a third time and missed. Then the deer got behind an apple tree and stopped where no shot was possible.

Hanson figured the buck's next move would be to head for the corn and he was ready to finish him when he did. But the whitetail fooled him. When the deer moved out from behind the screening apple tree, it headed toward some houses, preventing a shot.

Nonetheless, the buck was seriously hurt and left a good blood trail that Rick was able to follow to find his prize. Hanson stopped at the house to fill his wife in on what happened before recovering the whitetail. She was within earshot when he found the deer and put an insurance shot into it.

"I got him," Hanson hollered to his wife, so she would know the outcome. "He's a big one!"

"Everything happened so fast up until that time," Rick told me, "that I didn't have a chance to really look at the buck's rack. It was bigger than I thought. My wife came running over to look at it after she heard that I got it."

The buck had a dressed weight of 205 pounds and was aged at 4 1/2 or 5 1/2. Most of the bigger bucks that have been bagged in southern Michigan have been the same age. Craig Calderone's Jackson County 14-point was aged at 4 1/2 and had a dressed weight of 199.5 pounds. Troy Stephens' state record typical was 5 1/2 years old. Jackson County has produced a number of other B&C bucks besides the high ranking trio mentioned above and others are sure to be added to the list in the future.

It's interesting to note that the original net score for Hanson's buck was 185 1/8. It wasn't until almost a year after he got the deer that the final official net score of 188 1/8 was arrived at. Here's what happened.

Whitetail antlers can't be officially scored until after they air dry for at least 60 days. Once the drying period expired, Rick had the antlers from his buck measured by a CBM scorer who came up with a net score of 185 1/8. CBM rules require that the largest entries each year have to be panel measured before their score can be officially recorded. A panel of at least two scorers are required to verify measurements on the highest ranking racks.

The rack from Hanson's whitetail was not panel measured until September of 1998 at the Woods-N-Water Show in Imlay City. That's when the final official tally for the antlers was determined. The rack had a gross score of 193 4/8. Deductions for symmetry totaling 5 3/8 inches, resulted in the net score of 188 1/8. Greater beam and tine lengths is where the antlers picked up the higher score.

When initially scored, both beam lengths were listed as 25 6/8 inches. When panel measured, the right beam was found to be 26 2/8 inches long and the left was recorded as 26 1/8 inches in length. The left brow tine went from 7 1/8 to 8 5/8 inches.

CBM spokesperson Tira O'Brien said it is sometimes difficult to properly follow the curvature of beams and tines with a measuring tape to get the correct lengths. That's why most measurers use cables to determine those measurements. The fact that scores can vary from one measurer to another is the primary reason panel measuring is required for top ranking racks.

Michigan's Hanson Buck

The official score of Michigan's Hanson buck went from 185 1/8 to 188 1/8 after being panel measured at Woods-N-Water Weekend in Imlay City 10 months after the buck was bagged.

Mike Kelly with his impressive typical from Monroe County. It was his first buck. The 10-point measured 184 5/8. Photo courtesy Mike Kelly.

Chapter 9

Monroe County Monster

Borrowing a shotgun to hunt whitetails with is no guarantee that the borrower will bag a buck with a huge rack, but it may help. The fall of 1997 marked the second year in a row that a hunter who borrowed a shotgun to hunt with connected on one of the highest scoring typical bucks on record for Michigan. Troy Stephens from Jackson used a shotgun that was on loan to him from a friend during November of 1996 to shoot the number one typical on record for the state, a 16-pointer that scored 198.

The following November, Michael A. Kelly from Palm Beach Gardens, Florida used a shotgun he borrowed from a friend in Michigan to drop the second highest scoring typical known taken in the state for the year. The huge Monroe County 10-pointer will rank among the top 10 typicals in state records maintained by Commemorative Bucks of Michigan (CBM). The antlers from Kelly's buck had a final official score of 184 5/8.

The buck that Mike Kelly collected during the fall of 1997 was actually far more than he bargained for. He would have been happy with any antlered whitetail since he had never shot one before. That's right, the world class buck he got is the first one to his credit.

The Boone and Crockett qualifier was actually the second deer he shot. He got a doe a couple of years earlier. He almost got his first buck during the fall of 1996, but that one got away. He got his chance at that whitetail in the same place where he connected on the booner.

The fall of 1997 marked the fourth year of deer hunting for Kelly. He's a native of Michigan, but he didn't hunt deer while he lived in the state. It was after he moved to Florida that his interest in whitetail hunting prompted him to return.

Scott Smith from Milan is a friend of his and an avid deer hunter. Kelly made his first pilgrimage to Michigan for whitetail hunting with Smith during 1994 and he liked it so much that he made it an annual trip. While Mike hunts with Scott, he usually stays with another friend, Roger Meigasner.

Although Roger doesn't hunt, he owns a shotgun, and that's the gun Mike borrowed to hunt deer with. It's a 12 gauge Mossberg pump. The only sight it has is a bead at the end of the barrel. Mike usually loads it with Remington rifled slugs.

Kelly said he saw a lot of does during his first Michigan hunt, so he made sure to apply for an antlerless permit the second year and he was successful in drawing one of the tags. That's the year he shot the doe, which was his first whitetail. Although Mike didn't get a buck during his first two years of whitetail hunting in Michigan, he did see one that was a dandy, however, the timing made it impossible for him to take advantage of the opportunity.

"I was done hunting for the week during 1995 and was getting ready to go to the airport," Kelly said, "when I decided to go for a walk. I hadn't gone far when a doe went running by with a big 8-point buck right behind her. That buck may be the same one that I ended up shooting during 1997, but there's no way to know for sure.

"I didn't want to leave after seeing that buck, but I knew I had to go home. Seeing that buck made me that much more anxious to come back the following year. I was hooked on deer hunting in Michigan."

Mike was hoping for another glimpse of that buck or one like it, during his 1996 hunt. He was posted along the edge of a field when a 6-pointer appeared and he got excited. Kelly was a little too anxious to score and made too hasty a shot. Buck fever probably affected his aim, causing the slug to miss its mark.

He felt bad about that deer getting away, but the lesson he learned about the value of careful aiming before pulling the trigger had to play a role in his success on the trophy buck during 1997. Mike and Scott hunted a new area in Jackson County on opening day of the '97 season, but they failed to see any deer. Snowfall by the morning of the 16th, made driving conditions hazardous, so Kelly decided to hunt where he got the shot at the 6-point the year before.

"I plopped a folding chair down by a tree along the edge of a field," Mike said. "I sat 10 feet from the edge of the field, so trees would provide some cover, reducing the chances any deer that came along would see me. I don't think I sat any more than 45 minutes before I saw the buck.

"I thought it looked like a nice 8-point when he came walking out. There was snow on the ground and he really stood out in the open. He came out across the field heading toward some woods. He stopped on his own 70 yards away.

"I rested the shotgun against a tree and took careful aim. I wanted to make sure I didn't do the same thing that I did on the 6-pointer the year before. When I shot, he ran in the woods.

"When I got there, I was relieved to see he didn't go far. He only went 15 yards before collapsing. I made a good shot, getting him right through the lungs.

"After I got the buck, I called Scott right away. He said he would gut the buck and he did. He said it was an honor to do so."

Scott knows what a trophy buck looks like because he's taken one with antlers that score in the 160s. In fact, when Mike told him over the telephone that the buck he shot had antlers bigger than Scott's, Smith simply laughed. He didn't believe Kelly. His attitude obviously changed when he saw the whitetail where it fell.

The first words out of his mouth were, "Oh my God! You don't know what you've got here? This is a Boone and Crockett buck," and he was right. At the time, Mike Kelly didn't know the quality of the buck he got, inspite of his friend's reaction upon seeing its antlers. However, after several days of showing the buck around, it began to sink in. He had taken a whitetail of the caliber most deer hunters dream of seeing, but seldom do.

The buck was aged at 5 1/2 and it had a dressed weight of 199 pounds. The antlers are truly impressive, as the accompanying photos show.

Kelly's deer is the first in state records from Monroe County that has antlers large enough to qualify for national records maintained by Boone and Crockett. The minimum for entry of typical antlered whitetails in those records is 170. The highest scoring typical from that county prior to 1997, according to CBM records, was another 10-pointer measuring 167 2/8 that Frank Goble shot during the 1991 gun season.

Mike said he got his book buck near the Washtenaw County line. A number of booners have come from that county, including one larger than Kelly's. There is a possibility that some of the genetics that have been present in Washtenaw have spilled over into Monroe County. Time will tell.

Besides excellent tine length, the beams grown by the Kelly buck are long. The left beam is 28 inches long and the right is 29 2/8 inches in length. Inside spread between the beams is 23 5/8 inches.

Mike Kelly with his first buck and the borrowed shotgun he shot it with. Photo courtesy Mike Kelly.

Kenneth Montgomery with Clinton County 23-pointer measuring 212 2/8. He got the super buck from a hot spot that had produced a number of smaller bucks for him over the years. Photo courtesy Kenneth Montgomery.

Chapter 10

Biggest Nontypicals From 1997

A pair of exceptional bucks with nontypical racks were bagged on opening morning of the 1997 firearms season in Michigan and the antlers from both deer ended up scoring close to the same. Kenneth Montgomery from Lansing collected a 23-pointer in Clinton County that measured 212 2/8 and Bruce Maurer from Allegan connected on a 21-pointer in Allegan County that scored 210 4/8. Something else both of those successful hunters had in common is that the booners they bagged were shot from spots that had been consistent buck producers for them over the years.

By continuing to hunt their respective hot spots, each of these men managed to eventually claim world class bucks. It wasn't something they planned on doing or anticipated because the other bucks they had taken were small to average in size. It simply happened. The same thing can happen for you some day, if you've got a spot similar to the ones they were hunting.

Here are the stories behind their trophy bucks.

The Montgomery Buck

Kenneth Montgomery's deer was not only the highest scoring nontypical known taken in the state during '97, it's the number one nontypical on record for Clinton County, being the only rack of Boone and Crockett proportions currently listed in that category. The minimum score for entry in national records among nontypical gun kills is 195. The number one nontypical recorded for the county prior to '97 is a 15-pointer that John E. Daniels, Jr. shot during 1983. Those antlers measured 188 1/8.

Another booner with nontypical antlers that would have scored higher than Daniels' deer was taken in the county during 1963 by Ray Sadler of Grand Ledge, but he elected to enter it as a typical. Hunters who bag trophy bucks with a number of nontypical points have the option of listing them either as typicals or nontypicals.

When the nontypical score is significantly higher, most hunters choose to go with the higher number. In most cases, that will give the deer a higher ranking since far fewer nontypicals are entered than typicals.

The buck Sadler shot 34 years before Montgomery got his, had one more scorable point - 24. Inspite of the obvious nontypical structure of the rack, Ray opted for the typical score of 175 6/8 over the net nontypical tally of 202. The antlers qualify for B&C records either way (the minimum for typical gun kills in national records is 170), but there's a difference of 26 3/8 between those totals, which amounts to the combined lengths of all of the nontypical points.

Sadler said he decided to go with the typical score because the main frame was evenly matched. He added that the antlers had approximately 30 feet of smooth electrical wire wound around them at the time he shot the whitetail. That buck was the first one Ray ever shot.

The Sadler and Montgomery racks have something else in common besides the fact they are the only booners on record from Clinton County. Both deer that grew them were aged at 3 1/2. Considering the excellent antler development of those whitetails, it's amazing more booners haven't been bagged in the county. Perhaps more will show up in the future.

The booner that Ken shot was the 13th antlered whitetail he had taken from his favorite deer hunting spot. Those 13 bucks were taken over a span of nine years. A pair of 8-pointers and a 6 were the biggest deer he got at the site until 1997. Ken said one of the 8-points had antlers that were just over 18 inches wide and the other rack had a spread just under 18 inches.

The spot where Montgomery has met with such consistent success is a "hogsback" that's no more than 30 yards wide and 50 yards long in a big swamp. He said the swamp extends for more than a mile and provides important security cover for whitetails.

"The hogsback is nothing more than a patch of dry ground two feet higher than the rest of the swamp," Ken said. "There's always a lot of buck sign in the area. It's a good crossing spot for deer during gun season. If you don't see a buck there the first week, you're usually done. I've hunted that spot during muzzleloader season and not seen any bucks.

"The only year I didn't see a buck back there during gun season was around 1992 when a father and son did a lot of bowhunting in the area. It doesn't take long for deer to react to hunting pressure and move some where else."

Ken said he grew up on a farm as a boy and he did a lot of hunting then, but most of his efforts were directed at pheasants. He did some deer hunting back then, but not seriously. He managed to shoot a few does, but that was about it.

Montgomery got away from hunting for a number of years when he moved into the city. It wasn't until he returned to a rural setting in 1985 that he got back into hunting, especially for whitetails.

"That's when I learned to deer hunt," Ken said. "I learned to sit and wait for them to come to me instead of trying to go to them. When they come walking along and they don't know you're there is when you can get a good shot. Waiting in ambush is really the only way to hunt deer if you want to get a shot at them when they are undisturbed."

Since 1993, Ken has been hunting whitetails with a 12 gauge Remington 870 pump. It has a rifled barrel mounted with a 3-9 power scope. He shoots sabot slugs out of the gun, getting better accuracy than he used to with the smoothbore barrel on the Savage Slugger he formerly hunted with.

"I like the Remington shotgun," he said. "It's a nice gun. The action seems quieter than the Savage."

Montgomery first saw the huge buck he got on November 15, the day before gun season opened, which was a Saturday. He knew the rack was big at the time, but it turned out to be much bigger than he thought. The whitetail was about 100 yards away when Ken saw it following a doe. He didn't have binoculars handy to get the best view possible of the massive antlers.

"I figured the rack had 14 points and a 22-inch spread," Ken said. "The antlers actually had 23 points and the outside spread turned out to be 24 5/8 inches. It was impossible to see all of the points at that distance."

Although Montgomery knew the monster buck was in the area, he had no idea whether he would see the deer once the season opened. His hot spot was about a half mile from where he saw the deer the day before. The location had been too good to him over the years to hunt elsewhere, so he was on his hogsback when opening day arrived.

"A 4-point came through at 8:00 a.m.," Ken told me. "He had a really small rack, so I let him go. About an hour later I had two fawns in the brush feeding by me when a doe showed up. The big buck was following her.

"She came out in the open, but the buck stayed in the brush. She was coming right straight at me. I couldn't move. Meanwhile, I kept an eye on the buck and he was working his way toward the opening.

"When he finally broke into the clearing, I just swung my gun up and as soon as the crosshairs were on him, I fired. As soon as I moved, he stopped. When I shot, he wheeled in the brush and was gone. After he was gone I got to thinking, 'That was a wide rack.'"

Like so many hunters who have bagged some of Michigan's biggest bucks, Ken was in for the surprise of his life when he reached the fallen whitetail. He had been concentrating so hard on not spooking the antlerless deer that were near him and trying to get a shot at one that he knew had antlers, that he didn't have time to contemplate the size of the rack. He blood trailed the buck about 60 yards before finding it.

When Montgomery finally got a good look at the antlers, it didn't take him long to realize they were much bigger and wider than he dreamed possible. Inside spread

Bruce Maurer with his Allegan County nontypical scoring 210 4/8. The antlers have 21 points.

between the beams was 21 4/8 inches after the 60 day drying period. The beams were 25 7/8 and 26 inches long. Total length of nontypical points was 30 7/8 inches.

As mentioned earlier, the rack had an official net score of 212 2/8. The buck dressed out at 185 pounds. The DNR estimated the deer's age at 3 1/2.

The Maurer Buck

The first hours of the 1997 firearm deer season make up one morning that Bruce Maurer of Allegan will never forget. That's when he bagged the biggest buck he had ever seen during 33 years of deer hunting. The Allegan County whitetail's antlers proved to be bigger than most hunters in the state have seen and the rack was the second highest scoring nontypical known taken in the state during 1997 seasons.

The impressive antlers have a total of 21 scorable points that produced a net official score of 210 4/8, 5 4/8 inches less than the green score of 216 obtained soon after the deer was shot. Green score refers to unofficial measurements taken before a 60 day drying period has elapsed. Whitetail racks can't be officially scored for state and national records until after they have air dried for at least 60-days.

Maurer had the rack officially measured on February 7, 82 days after the deer was shot. Some shrinkage usually occurs during the drying period, as is obvious by the differences between the green and official measurements. Nonetheless, the antlers will end up with a high ranking in state records and will easily qualify for national records maintained by the Boone and Crockett Club. The minimum for entry in national records is 195 and nontypical gun kills only have to score 150 to be listed in state records compiled by Commemorative Bucks of Michigan (CBM).

According to CBM Records, the Maurer head ranks as the second highest scoring nontypical for Allegan County. A 30-pointer that Jon West bagged in that county during the 1984 gun season measured 231 1/8. The former number two nontypical from the county was a 20-pointer Jason Newman collected with bow and arrow in 1994. Those antlers scored 195 4/8.

On a statewide basis, the final score puts Maurer's buck in the top 20 among nontypicals on CBM's alltime records list at the time this was written.

Bruce bagged his book buck in a spot that he had been hunting for the previous 12 years. Each year, he sat in the same place on a stool next to a large tree to wait for deer to come by. And he had good reason to expect bucks to pass within view. There are well used deer trails visible from Maurer's chosen stand site and some of the trees along those trails are always rubbed by passing bucks.

The fact that Bruce had taken four bucks while posted in that spot during previous seasons, boosted his confidence in the location. He said he hadn't been very successful in seeing bucks until he started hunting that location. The biggest of the four he got previously was an 8-pointer that dressed out at 154 pounds. He got that whitetail nine years earlier and had a head mount made from the deer to put on his wall.

Amazingly, that 8-pointer was only 1 1/2 years old. Both its antler and body size were exceptional for a buck of that age. In the years that followed, Bruce bagged three more yearling bucks from the spot, all of which had smaller antlers than the one he had mounted. One had 5 points, another 6 and the third had 8 points.

Maurer said he's normally in position by 6:30 a.m. on mornings he plans on hunting and that's when he arrived at his favorite spot on opening day of the '97 season. A fresh coating of five inches of snow on the ground, something deer hunters in southern Michigan don't often have early in the season, increased visibility on November 15. He saw his first deer that morning between 7:30 and 7:45. A group of eight does walked by about 20 yards away.

About an hour later, Bruce saw a whitetail walking from right to left about 70 yards away. Through the trees, he made out the tips of antlers off to the sides of the deer's head, so he knew it was a buck, and he immediately shouldered his Mossberg 12 gauge pump to prepare for a shot. The whitetail went out of sight and he kept watching where he expected it to reappear. The deer must have stopped when it disappeared from his view because minutes ticked by slowly before he saw it again. However, he worried that the buck might have turned and was gone for good, before it reappeared.

Bruce figured about five minutes elapsed before he saw the deer again. He still had his shotgun up. Once he confirmed it was the buck, he concentrated on looking at the kill zone through the 2X7 power variable scope mounted on his shotgun. As soon as he was on target, he pulled the trigger, sending a Remington slug toward the whitetail.

When the buck disappeared from view again, Maurer assumed he missed. Soon after the buck disappeared, Bruce saw a number of deer running, some of which may have been the does he saw earlier, but he thought one of the fleeing whitetails was the one he shot at. He waited where he was for a half hour before going to the spot where the buck had been when he shot to try to confirm what happened.

He was pleasantly surprised to find the huge deer piled up where it had been standing when he shot. It had dropped in its tracks instantly, explaining why it disappeared so fast. Up until that point, Bruce knew the buck that he shot at had antlers, but he wasn't sure how big they were. He had seen four points on one beam, so he guessed it was probably another 8-pointer. However, he had no idea of the rack's true size until he saw the lifeless carcass.

"I was shocked when I saw it," he said. "I just couldn't believe how big the antlers were. I've been hunting that spot for 12 years and never saw anything that big before."

Although Maurer had never seen the deer before, he later found out from someone who lives near where Bruce hunted, that he had seen the whitetail during the summer. Bruce said this person owns 70 acres of land on which he doesn't allow any hunting. Maurer said he suspected there was at least one big buck in the area, based on the big trees that were rubbed. However, he assumed that it stayed on the private refuge until after dark.

That may very well be how the buck lived as long as it did. It was estimated to be 5 1/2 years old and had a dressed weight of 203 pounds. One or more hot does were probably responsible for the buck's appearance in front of Maurer.

One of the things that really helped boost the score on Bruce's buck were the length of its main beams. The rack had the longest beams of any buck in state records at the time it was entered, according to CBM Records Keeper Tira O'Brien. The right beam was 31 inches long and the left beam measured 29 2/8 inches.

The inside spread between the beams was also greater than normal at 21 inches. Mass of the antlers was exceptional, too. The right beam had a six-inch circumference at the base and the left antler measured 5 5/8 inches below the brow tine.

There was also good tine length. The longest tine on the left side was 11 6/8 inches long and the longest point on the right side was 10 7/8 inches. The rack had a total of 10 nontypical points with combined measurements of 21 inches.

Bruce said he continued hunting his hot spot later in the season and he saw a 6-pointer he could have shot on Thanksgiving morning. However, his son was hunting with him that day and he hadn't bagged a buck yet, so he tried to chase the whitetail toward his son. Unfortunately, the effort didn't work. However, Maurer wasn't disappointed he didn't shoot what would have been his second buck for the season. Afterall, he was more than satisfied with taking Michigan's second best nontypical for the year!

As Maurer and Montgomery found out, persistence pays when it comes to whitetail hunting. The more time you spend in a spot that consistently produces bucks, the better your chances of eventually taking a trophy animal. Of course, it helps if you pass up some of the smaller bucks, too, as Ken Montgomery did. If he had shot the forkhorn he saw first on opening day of the 1997 season, there's an excellent chance he might not have gotten the state's highest scoring nontypical that year. Not that morning, at any rate.

Chuck Conaway with his first bow kill on his first day of bowhunting. The 10-point scores 172 7/8. Brother-in-law Zane Walker played an important role in Conaway's success. Photo courtesy Chuck Conaway.

Chapter 11

Beginner's Luck Booner

The lifetime goal of many bowhunters who try their luck on whitetails is to get a shot at a buck with a Boone and Crockett rack. Charles Conaway from East Greenwich, Rhode Island did it on his first afternoon in a tree stand while hunting in Michigan and he made good on the opportunity. With barely three hours of bowhunting under his belt, he had his first buck and it was a booner!

Conaway had no idea how good a buck he was drawing on at the time, of course, and it's a good thing he didn't. If he would have known the buck was the biggest he is likely to see regardless of how many more years he hunts, it could have had a profound effect on his ability to make the shot.

"I knew the buck was big," Chuck told me, "but I didn't realize how big until starting to show the deer to people who are experienced bowhunters the next day. Not in my wildest dream did I think it was of Pope and Young caliber, much less Boone and Crockett. I never thought I could ever be that lucky."

The beginning bowhunter was obviously incredibly lucky to take such a tremendous trophy during his first attempt at bowhunting. However, there was a considerable amount of planning and preparation that went into his success. The fact that he scored on the first time he sat in a tree stand was no accident. All bowhunters, whether novice or veteran, can do the same thing by following the same formula that contributed to Conaway's success.

The first time any stand is occupied is when it's most often likely to produce results, if it is set up properly and the timing is right. The buck or bucks seen from a fresh stand will seldom be as large as the one Chuck shot. For that matter, many archers are satisfied with an antlerless deer. So the first time you sit in a stand should offer the best chance of taking any deer.

A lot of the credit for Chuck's success goes to his brother-in-law Zane Walker from North Branch. Incidentally, Conaway arrowed his booner in Lapeer County.

Although Chuck now lives and works in Rhode Island, he grew up in Michigan and that's where he returned for his first bowhunt with Walker. Conaway's brother-in-law is an experienced bowhunter who selected the spot for his stand along with friend Doug Muxlow, who is also a veteran bowhunter.

Zane and Doug, who each had more than 15 years of experience bowhunting for whitetails at the time, put the stand up four days before Chuck's arrival. The stand was placed 20 to 25 feet from the ground overlooking a creek crossing that was getting a lot of use. Buck sign was abundant in the area. Zane said there were five scrapes in the vicinity and a lot of antler rubs, including some on trees as big around as his thigh.

Chuck's brother-in-law also helped decide the best timing for Conaway's hunt. Walker knew that some of the biggest bucks in the state have been consistently bagged during early November, with the 5th through the 8th being prime time. That's also the best timing for seeing bucks of any size as the rut starts to crank up. Chuck planned his hunt to start November 8th and that's the day he got his buck of a lifetime.

As experienced deer hunters, both Zane and Doug are interested in trophy bucks and they usually set stands up in locations where they think their chances of scoring on a good buck are best. Doug had taken a nice whitetail that netted around 120 during the first week of October. Zane did even better on October 16th with a 9-pointer that netted 140 4/8, easily qualifying for a spot in Pope and Young and state records.

Zane said the weather was warm on the day he got his book buck, with a temperature of about 75. The weather was so nice, he figured it was perfect for sitting in a tree stand. After he was in the stand, he decided to try some rattling. He rattled once and the whitetail came to investigate as he set the antlers down.

Although November 8th, 1996 marked Chuck Conaway's first day of bowhunting, it wasn't his first day of whitetail hunting. He had hunted deer with a shotgun from the time he was a boy through college. He shot a lot of bucks with a gun on the property where he bowhunted that fall. The biggest ones had 8 and 10-point racks, but none of the antlers were exceptional.

By the time Chuck decided to try bowhunting, it had been 12 years since he had shot a whitetail. He bought a Browning bow with a 65 pound draw weight about a week before his hunt in Michigan. He had a local archery shop set the bow up for him.

Zane made some adjustments to Chuck's bow when he arrived in Michigan to improve its performance. To make sure Chuck could shoot the bow and Easton Super Slam arrows as good as possible, they spent the morning of November 8th practicing rather than hunting. With Zane's coaching, it wasn't long before Chuck was shooting consistently with the Vortex broadheads he planned to hunt with.

It was 3:00 p.m. when the beginning bowhunter climbed into the tree stand overlooking the creek crossing. Almost three hours later, the sun was starting to set when three does crossed the creek. Chuck was concentrating on the does when he heard what he thought were frogs croaking. What he at first thought were frogs proved to be a buck grunting as he followed the does, one of which may have been in heat.

"As the buck approached, all I could think about is, 'How am I going to get this bow back,'" Chuck told me.

Despite his concern, he managed to come to full draw with no problem. To his advantage, the buck was concentrating on the does and had no idea a human was within miles. When the whitetail was 15 yards away and broadside, Conaway took his shot.

"As soon as I released the arrow, I knew it was a good shot," Chuck said. "I aimed behind the buck's shoulder and that's where the arrow hit. I got him through both lungs."

Conaway didn't attempt to locate the buck after making the shot. He waited until he met up with Zane and they both went to trail the deer.

Zane Walker with a 9-pointer scoring 140 4/8 that he bagged on October 16, 1996. Photo courtesy Zane Walker.

Zane Walker with the book buck he got during December of 1996 with bow and arrow. Photo courtesy Zane Walker.

"Chuck told me, 'I shot a real nice buck and it's bigger than yours,'" Walker told me. "I said, 'Ya, right, and chuckled. I thought he was pulling my leg or exaggerating. Boy, was I in for a surprise when we got to the deer. It only went about 100 yards from where he shot it.

"The antlers were huge," Zane continued. "I thought they could be big enough to make Boone and Crockett and they were. The gross score of the antlers was 177 1/8 and they netted 172 7/8."

"The 10-pointer's neck was huge, just like a horse," Chuck added. "It had a dressed weight of 224 pounds and was 5 1/2 years old. I was just at the right place at the right time. It's better to be lucky than good, I guess."

It's actually best to be both lucky and good, which more accurately describes what happened in Chuck's case. Zane helped him master his bow and put a tree stand in place for him, enabling Chuck to be good enough to take advantage of the opportunity at the book buck when it came along. There was an excellent chance Chuck was going to see a buck from the stand he bowhunted from. Where the luck came in is that it was a whitetail of Boone and Crockett proportions.

Since there is a two deer bag limit in Michigan, Chuck continued hunting after he got his booner. He saw two spikehorns on the 9th, but didn't shoot either one of them. Chuck ended up returning to Michigan for Thanksgiving, when gun season was underway, and filled his second buck tag with a 5-pointer that he got with a shotgun.

Zane managed to take a second Pope and Young buck with bow and arrow during Michigan's late bow season in December. It was the day after Christmas and his objective that day was actually to collect a doe for a relative of his who wanted some venison. He was in the process of walking from one end of the property to the other when he saw a pair of does jump a fence.

It wasn't long before a buck appeared "bird dogging" the does where they crossed a field before they jumped the fence. Zane was wearing Mossy oak snow camo, so he hunkered down along the fenceline and waited for the buck to get within bow range. He took his shot when the whitetail was about 25 yards away. The 8-pointer netted 129 3/8.

An Example From The U.P.

Steve Gorsuch from Sault Ste. Marie also proved you don't have to be an experienced bowhunter to bag a big buck in Michigan during the 1989 season. He bagged a whitetail with the highest scoring nontypical rack known taken in the state that year. The antlers weren't of Boone and Crockett proportions in this case, but they were close. The 20-point rack scored 186 6/8.

The fall of 1989 was not actually Gorsuch's first attempt at bowhunting. He spent a few days in the field with bow and arrow during 1988, trying to shoot a whitetail, but was unsuccessful. Steve received the necessary equipment to become a bowhunter as

Christmas gifts from his wife during '88.

After becoming familiar with his bow, he managed to hunt with it on three or four days during December. The novice archer spent most of his time walking and never got close enough to a deer for a good shot. As a result of his experience with bow and arrow, he realized his best chance of success would be to let the deer come to him rather than trying to walk within range of one.

So, with the help of brother-in-law John Morningstar, Steve built a tree stand before the 1989 bow deer season opened. He also did a lot of practice with his archery equipment to prepare for the October 1 opener. Steve even put a bale of hay with a target on it 10 yards from his tree stand, so he could practice from the platform.

The platform was positioned 12 feet above the ground between a clump of three maple trees. He added a rear view mirror to his blind so he could watch a deer trail behind him.

Gorsuch was in his tree stand before daylight on opening day. The platform he occupied and the equipment in his hands wasn't all that was new either. He was hunting deer for the first time on a parcel of property in Mackinac County that he had purchased during the year.

Never having hunted from a tree stand before, Steve described his first experience as, "One of the eeriest feelings I've ever had. I didn't enjoy my first two hours in the blind," he said. "That all changed when I heard my first deer coming."

Two does appeared about 8:30 a.m. and started feeding on sugar beets he had been using for bait. Gorsuch said he decided to try for one of the deer, but his arrow fell off of the rest as he pulled the string. It made a noise when he put it back in place, alerting the whitetails. He finally got a shot though and his arrow went low.

Before leaving his blind for the morning, Steve took three practice shots with his 52 pound pull Pro Line bow and they all struck low. His sight pin had moved somehow and he readjusted it so his arrows hit where he was aiming.

With renewed confidence, he returned to his tree stand at 3:30 p.m. Three hours later, he heard a deer approaching. When the animal finally came into view he saw that it was a big buck.

This time his Satellite-tipped arrow was on target. Steve said he had no idea a buck of that caliber was in the area, although he had seen some buck sign the day before bow season opened. He found a good antler rub and a scrape about 100 yards from his blind.

If it hadn't been for the missed shot at the doe in the morning, alerting the hunter to a possible problem with his sight pin, his shot at the buck might have missed instead. If Steve had collected the doe during the morning, of course, he certainly wouldn't have gotten the buck because his tag would have been filled. Gorsuch has no complaints about the circumstances that led him to his trophy buck.

Steve Gorsuch with his first bow buck from Mackinac County, a 20-pointer scoring 186 6/8.

Bob Mechon with 8 1/2-year-old buck that his parents named Lucky. Bob's father fed the buck during the winter. The whitetail normally didn't arrive in the area until after hunting season ended. Photo courtesy Joe Mechon.

Chapter 12

A Buck Named Lucky

Bob Mechon from Union Town, Ohio has shot plenty of bucks in Michigan's Upper Peninsula over the years, which is where he was born and raised, but none were as special as a trophy whitetail he bagged on November 20, 1994 in Iron County. The size and age of the buck were enough to make the deer stand out in most people's eyes. The 10-pointer was 8 1/2 years old when it was shot and it weighed 246 pounds in the round. After field dressing, the carcass tipped the scales at 193 pounds.

Few antlered whitetails live as long as that one did in the state or attain that size. Although the deer had a big set of antlers when it was killed, one the majority of hunters would be pleased to get, the rack was not as large as many other bucks that reach the age it did. In fact, the antlers weren't quite large enough to qualify for state records maintained by Commemorative Bucks of Michigan (CBM).

As a typical, the rack had a gross score of 137 4/8, but with 13 3/8 inches of deductions, the final net score was 124 1/8. Bucks with typical racks taken with firearms must score at least 125 to make it into state records. As a nontypical, the antlers netted 142 7/8, and the CBM minimum for that category is 150.

But antler size and score are only one way to measure a trophy whitetail. Other qualities are sometimes more important. In this case, the buck's age is certainly a consideration. It takes a wise deer to avoid getting shot as long as that one did. What really made that buck special besides its size, age and wisdom is Mechon knew a lot of the antlered whitetail's history thanks to his father's winter deer feeding program.

Joe Mechon from Amasa is Bob's father. Joe and his wife Edith live in a rural setting, with a variety of wildlife nearby, including deer. When Joe retired, he started a winter deer feeding program as a hobby. He and his family enjoy watching whitetails. The U.P.'s tough winters also motivated Joe to begin feeding deer. He wanted to help some of the local deer make it through critical winter months.

The buck that Bob shot during November of 1994 was first observed at the Mechon

Estates, taking advantage of Joe's handouts, during 1988. The deer had a 6-point rack and was estimated to be 1 1/2 years old, but he could have been 2 1/2. A second buck that was smaller and had 5-point antlers, also took advantage of the feeding program. The two bucks spent a lot of time together during the winter of 1988-89.

The 6-pointer's antlers added two more tines when he grew a new set during 1989. The number of points on the whitetail's rack remained the same over the next two years, but the beams got heavier and the tines became longer. The buck that had been a 5-pointer, became a 6 the next year and then an 8.

The bucks showed up at the Mechon Homestead each year within a few days after hunting season ended and left when spring arrived, usually during April. It was as though they knew when it was safe to come out of hiding. They were safe at the Mechon's feeding area any time, but there were hunters nearby who would have shot the bucks, if they got the chance.

Joe is a deer hunter himself, but he hadn't killed a whitetail in years during the mid-1990s. He still bought a deer license every year anyway and carried a rifle in the woods, according to Edith, but she said that's the extent of it. If he were to shoot a deer, it would be no where near his home.

Bob sometimes hunts near the homestead, but he tries to pass up bucks that he knows are feeding in his parents' yard. He never saw the two bucks that became regular winter visitors while hunting anyway - until 1994 - because they didn't arrive until hunting season ended.

During the normal course of events, the pair of bucks that became annual visitors to the Mechon Homestead were named. They both had 8-point racks by 1990 and names made it easier for Joe and Edith to know which deer they were talking about. The bigger 8-pointer was named Lucky and the second deer was referred to as Bucky.

By 1992, Lucky became a 9-pointer when the second tine on the right beam forked. That was the first set of antlers shed by either buck that Joe managed to find. Lucky lost the antlers during January and Joe found the right side soon afterward.

He didn't come across the left beam until late February when rain melted enough snow to expose it. That antler had only been dropped about 40 feet from its mate, but it sank deep enough in the snow to obscure it from view. Lucky was 6 1/2 years old during 1992 and the rack he grew that year scored 109 1/8, based on an estimated inside spread of 16 inches.

The right beam was 21 inches long and the left beam was 19 6/8 inches in length. The circumference of the right beam was 4 2/8 inches compared to a measurement of 4 1/8 inches on the left side. The third point on each beam was the longest, measuring 8 3/8 inches on the right and 9 2/8 inches on the left.

Lucky remained a 9-pointer in 1993 and Joe was lucky enough to find the sheds from that year, too. As a 7 1/2-year-old, the buck's antlers were still growing. With a similar inside spread as the year before, the antlers measured 123. All measurements were greater than the year before.

The beams were 21 7/8 and 22 1/8 inches in length. Circumferences of both

A Buck Named Lucky

Lucky with the 8-point rack he grew during 1991 when 5 1/2 years old. Photo courtesy Joe Mechon.

beams was 4 3/8 inches. The third tines were 8 2/8 and 10 1/8 inches long.

More importantly, Lucky's timing was off during 1993. For the first time since he had been visiting the Mechon's property, he arrived before deer season ended. He was so comfortable there, that he started taking advantage of the supplemental food earlier than normal. Part of the reason for the change in behavior is the buck might have lost more weight than normal during rutting activities and was hungry. The older bucks get, the more dominant they become and the more active a role they play during the breeding season.

Bucky's timing was obviously off that year, too. He was shot during the third day of firearms season in the vicinity of the Mechon's Estate.

At the time, none of the Mechons realized the change in Lucky's behavior during 1993 was a sign of even more of a change to come the following year. There's no way they could have known.

On the morning of November 20, 1994, Bob was hunting near the homestead when he saw a big buck chasing a doe. He saw antlers, but because the deer was moving in an out of cover and through the trees, he wasn't able to get a clear picture of the rack. Joe said he heard the two shots from Bob's .270.

Like most fathers who pass the hunting tradition on to their sons, Joe considered the shots a good sign. He was confident his son had gotten a buck and felt good about it. That attitude didn't change when he found out Bob shot Lucky.

Sure, Joe would have preferred that Bob would have gotten a different big buck, but he also knew that the buck he had been watching and feeding every winter since 1988 had lived a good life that was much longer than most Michigan whitetails. As a hunter himself, he knew that it was amazing that some one else hadn't bagged the special buck before then. If any one were to shoot the deer, Joe felt better about his son doing so than some one else and not knowing what happened.

Like most deer kills, there's normally a feeling of sadness mixed with the pleasure of success. The feeling of remorse or regret was simply stronger in this case, especially for Bob. If he had known it was Lucky chasing the doe, he probably would not have shot it. It was a surprise to everyone that Lucky was in the area so early.

Lucky's final set of antlers has 10 points. The second tine on the left beam forked for the first time like the one on the right side had the previous two years. The two nontypical points made a significant contribution to the 13 3/8 inches of deductions to arrive at the net typical score of 124 1/8. The nontypical point on the right side was 6 1/8 inches long compared to 3 2/8 inches for the nontypical tine on the left side.

By 1994, Lucky's main beams were 21 6/8 and 22 2/8 inches long. Circumferences of the beams were 4 4/8 inches. The third points were 9 6/8 and 10 2/8 inches long.

Bob had Taxidermist Tom Rankin from Hartville, Ohio do a head mount of the special buck and put it on a display with his shed antlers from the two previous years. What remains of the buck are just as special to the Mechons as when the deer was alive.

A Buck Named Lucky

Bob Mechon with Lucky and the shed antlers the whitetail grew the two previous years. Photo courtesy Joe Mechon.

Rock Vore with the head mount of the trophy buck he and his brother spotted from a road and successfully stalked with bow and arrow. The 11-point rack netted 180 2/8.

Chapter 13

Oakland County Booner

There's no better example of the unpredictability of trophy buck hunting than the amazing success of Rock Vore of Highland during the fall of 1994. It's simply impossible to know when, where, how or if any hunter will get the chance of a lifetime at a world class whitetail buck. That chance often comes when it's least expected and if you don't identify it or take advantage of it, you may have missed the chance of a lifetime.

Vore proved that if you're serious about taking a trophy buck, it pays to be vigilant at all times, even when you're not hunting. A clue or a deer sighting that you encounter at any time can eventually lead the observant hunter down the road to success. In some cases, the road can be a long one and in others, it's short.

Tagging a trophy buck was probably the furthest thing from Rock's mind when the circumstances developed for him to collect one of the highest scoring typical bucks taken by a bowhunter in the state. He wasn't even hunting at the time, although he was thinking about it. It wasn't a pleasant day to be hunting anyway. Rain was falling and it was very windy.

Rock and older brother Scott were on their way home after returning a hunting video to Tree Stand Archery. They decided to take the long way home to look for deer in an area where they had seen whitetails before. They didn't have any hunting equipment with them. Like most hunters, they simply like to see deer any time they can. Sightings are often filed away to be checked out during future scouting missions or hunts.

It was 1:00 p.m. on November 6th when Scott suddenly said, "Look at that monster buck!"

Rock knew the deer had to be something special through the excitement in his brother's voice. The word "monster" also caught his attention. He said he had heard Scott refer to bucks as "big" numerous times in the past, but never monsters.

Rock was driving, so he went by the buck before he had the chance to see it. He quickly stopped and backed up to get a look at the whitetail that had captured his brother's attention. The view he got confirmed Scott's assessment.

What's amazing is the buck was bedded in a cattail swamp only about 50 yards from the road and it remained where it was while the brothers stared at it in disbelief from their stationary vehicle. Big bucks that live along roads frequently ignore vehicles that drive on by, but bolt at the instant one stops. Apparently, this one felt secure where he was.

Rock said the trophy buck was bedded in a marsh where it blended well with its surroundings. If it weren't for Scott's experience in spotting deer, they probably wouldn't have seen it. Although the animal was tough to see, Scott made the identification immediately, something other motorists traveling that road that day probably failed to do.

If the buck had been on private land the pair didn't have access to, that would be the end of the story. The same thing would have been true if they felt the deer was unapproachable and went home hoping the whitetail might wander by one of their tree stands some day. But they did have access to the land where the buck was because it was owned by the state and they thought they had a good chance of sneaking within bow range of the deer. The weather certainly favored a stalk.

The brothers hustled home as quickly as possible, donning camo clothes and grabbing their archery equipment, intent on stalking the buck of a lifetime. One of their main concerns was that the whitetail would be gone by the time they got back. They also had thoughts of other hunters seeing the deer and trying for it. If that happened, they would surely spook the buck out of the area, if they weren't successful in shooting it.

Needless to say, the Vores were relieved when the whitetail was still there upon their return and there was no sign of other hunters. They didn't stop within view of the deer like they had before, simply cruising by to make sure they weren't wasting their time to put their sneak attack into action. They continued on around to a point about 300 yards from where the buck was bedded to start their stalk. That position enabled them to move into the wind as well as approach the buck from the rear.

They knew they were going to get wet. Besides the falling rain, water clung to all the vegetation and there was standing water in the swamp. They didn't mind the discomfort as long as they were able to get within bow range of their quarry. Rain gear was out of the question because it would be too noisy.

The water was actually one of their allies. It would make their approach quieter and help cover any noise they did make.

Rock was carrying a 72 pound pull Darton Woodsman bow during the stalk. His XX75 aluminum arrows were tipped with Muzzy broadheads. Scott had a Browning Mirage bow set at 75 pounds that he hoped to shoot the buck with.

Both bowhunters were experienced, having started when they were 12 years old, the minimum age at which boys and girls can begin bowhunting for big game in

Michigan. Rock was 30 when he got his trophy buck and Scott was 37, so they had 18 and 25 years of bowhunting experience respectively by 1994. Recurve bows were still popular when Scott started bowhunting.

Like so many other Michigan deer hunters, the first buck Rock bagged was taken with a firearm rather than bow and arrow. He was hunting near Evart during the 1985 season at the age of 21 when he connected on a beautiful 11-pointer that would score between 110 and 120. It was early in the season when he went to a ground blind that his grandfather had constructed with a view of a horseshoe-shaped swamp.

Vore said he was only in the blind about 15 minutes when the buck appeared about 50 yards away in the swamp and he dropped it with a .35 caliber rifle. He commented that claiming his first buck with such a nice rack was a thrill he will never forget.

Bowhunting is tougher to master than gun hunting since you have to be so much closer for a shot with archery tackle. The keen senses that whitetails possess makes it difficult to get the ideal bow shot, consequently, it usually takes much longer to connect with an arrow than a bullet or slug. But bowhunting has so many other rewards than a filled tag, which keep Rock and plenty of other archers like him trying. By being persistent, Vore eventually scored with archery equipment.

Prior to '94, both Rock and Scott had taken a number of whitetails with arrows. Scott had bow-bagged more deer than his younger brother, but the bucks he tagged had been young ones. Rock's first antlered whitetail taken with bow and arrow, on the other hand, had been a real dandy with 9 points and a 19 1/2-inch spread. The rack from that buck would certainly qualify for a spot in state records, too, but Vore didn't have it measured. The mature whitetail had a dressed weight of 196 pounds after hanging for three days.

On the day Rock arrowed the 9-pointer, which was October 27th, 1990, he was in a tree stand along the edge of a field before first light. He said he put some Tink's 69 scent in a nearby scrape before climbing into the stand. Soon after it was light enough to see, the buck appeared. It smelled the scent Rock put out and stopped to paw the ground there before coming closer. The whitetail was only 10 yards from his tree, angling away, when he released an arrow from his 68 pound pull Darton Thunderhead bow.

Although Rock started bowhunting when he was 12, he said he didn't get serious about it until 1985. His first kills were does taken in 1988 and '89 and he got the 9-pointer the following year. Small bucks or does had fallen to his arrows since then.

Vore's 1994 tag almost went on a forkhorn. He got a shot at that deer on October 25, but his arrow missed. Instead, a tremendous 11-pointer with a final net score of 180 2/8 fell to one of his arrows. He said he never expected to get a buck with antlers that big. He and his brother knew the rack was big when they started stalking the animal, but they didn't realize the antlers were THAT BIG!

The brothers stayed as low as possible as they snuck toward the biggest buck either of them had ever seen. They figured that would reduce their chances of being seen. The pair also moved slowly to prevent making any more noise than necessary. During part of the stalk, they had to crawl through swamp water on their knees.

The bowhunters had the spot carefully marked where the buck was bedded. Since the whitetail was facing into the wind, they were able to stalk toward the animal from behind it most of the time. It took them two hours of slow, painstaking crawling to get close enough to try a shot. The brothers ended up about 25 yards from the deer and they maneuvered into position for a shot with the deer angling away from them.

They both drew their bows and shot at about the same time. Scott's arrow missed, but Rock's connected, entering in front of the hind quarter and angled forward into the lungs. The buck jumped to its feet when hit, but only made it 20 yards before going down for keeps.

They were a pair of very happy, wet bowhunters at that point. They deserve a lot of credit for being skillful enough to get as close as they did without alerting the buck. However, the wind and rain played a critical role in their success, too. If the weather conditions had been different, there's an excellent chance the buck would have sensed their presence before they got a shot.

Rock said the buck had a dressed weight of 203 pounds and its age was estimated at 5 1/2. At the time the deer was taken, the inside spread of the antlers was 18 6/8 inches and there were 12 official points. The rack has 10 typical points and there were two stickers, one near the base of the right beam and another over an inch long off of a tine on the left side. Both sticker points were deductions on his green score, giving the rack a gross score of 187 7/8 and a net of 179 6/8.

However, after the required 60-day drying period, the sticker point on the right beam had shrunk enough to end up less than an inch and was no longer considered in the score, giving the antlers a final tally over 180. Points have to measure at least an inch to count.

The rack's long tines really boosted the score. Four of the points are over 12 inches long and one is 13 1/8 inches in length. The beams were also long, each taping more than 27 inches.

It's a buck any bowhunter would be proud of and the only reason this Michigan archer managed to bag it is he capitalized on a chance encounter that he never expected to occur. If there's any lesson to be learned from Rock's success, it's to always keep your eyes open, whether or not you're hunting, because you never know where, when or how that buck of a lifetime might appear. It also pays to be versatile and willing to go the extra mile to help take advantage of an opportunity when ever it does occur. If Rock and Scott had decided not to try a stalk on that buck because it was too wet or they figured it wouldn't work, that buck might have ended up with some one else's tag on it!

Oakland County Booner

Rock Vore with one of the state's best bow kills that he got by taking advantage of a unique opportunity when it was least expected. Photo courtesy Rock Vore.

*Senior citizen Jack Eddy with head mounts of a pair of book bucks he bagged on November 15, 1998. The fact that he has to use a walker to get around during recent years hasn't stopped him from taking trophy bucks.
Photo courtesy Jack Van Riper.*

Chapter 14

Expert Senior Citizen

Jack Eddy from Owosso is one of Michigan's most successful senior citizen big buck hunters, relying on firearms to take his trophy whitetails. He has a total of 22 deer from seven counties in state records maintained by Commemorative Bucks of Michigan (CBM), 17 of which he's taken since 1989 when he was 65 years old. He has nine entries from Saginaw County and seven from Gratiot County, two from Kalkaska County and one each from Shiawassee, Calhoun, Crawford and the U.P.'s Houghton County.

The antlers from each of those 22 bucks score at least 125 since that's the minimum for listing of typical gun kills in state records. Two of those 22 was entered as nontypicals. The CBM minimum for nontypical gun kills is 150. Many of the bucks Eddy entered in the records measure much higher than the minimums.

The trophy whitetails he bagged during 1995 and '97 are perfect examples. His 1995 entry is a 13-point nontypical scoring 162 6/8 that he got in Gratiot County. That was the first nontypical on record for the county. While hunting the same spot during 1997, he shot a 10-point typical that measured 155 4/8, putting it in the number two spot among typicals for the county.

He passed up shots at each of those bucks the year before he got them. In the case of the 10-pointer scoring 155 4/8, he actually passed it up two years before he tagged it. When he saw the nontypical during 1994, for instance, it simply stuck its head out of a thick patch of cover. Not wanting to risk damaging the rack, he held his fire, hoping the deer would step out in the open, but it didn't. Eddy eventually settled for an 8-pointer from the area during '94 that scored 140 6/8. He got an even bigger buck from Saginaw County that fall, an 11-pointer that measured 156 6/8.

Although Jack didn't kill the nontypical whitetail that day during 1994 that he saw it, the sighting turned him onto the buck's "hidey hole," setting the stage for taking him in '95. Eddy scouted the thick patch of cover that the deer's head emerged from and discovered it was the flood plain for a stream. Tag alders and young oak trees that were almost impenetrable grew on the 50-yard-wide flood plain. Deer beds like bathtubs and huge tracks measuring 3 1/2 inches were in the security cover.

The experienced hunter figured if the trophy buck didn't want to leave the thick cover and come to him, he would go to the deer. He selected a spot for a blind in the thick stuff and cut three shooting lanes. That's where he was on November 15, 1995.

Jack knew the nontypical was still in the area and that's the one he wanted, so he passed up two other bucks before getting a shot at the 13-pointer. One of the bucks he let go was a small 8-point and the other was a 9-point that he figured would score in the 130s. Even though the 9 would have qualified for state records, passing on it was obviously a good choice because the deer had a much bigger rack when he did shoot it in 1997.

Eddy said he first saw the nontypical around 10:00 a.m. on opening morning of the '95 season when it entered the ribbon of cover along the stream in the distance. It was six hours later at 4:00 p.m. when the buck finally made its way to one of the waiting hunter's shooting lanes. The whitetail was probably bedded for much of the time after Jack originally saw it until he dropped it with his .270. The buck was 8 1/2 years old and weighed 240 pounds in the round.

A return to the same blind before daylight on opening day of the 1997 season was also well rewarded. Based on detailed preseason scouting, Jack knew the 9-pointer he passed two years earlier had a much bigger rack by then and was the dominant buck in the area. That deer was his target.

At 73 years of age then, Eddy wasn't getting around as good as he used to. He used a walker to help him get to his blind. Soon after daylight, a 10-pointer that would have scored about 110 and a 7-point jumped a nearby fence and disappeared in the thick cover. After 9:30 a.m., Jack noticed chickadees bouncing around in one place in the thicket. He looked the area over thoroughly with the scope on his rifle and eventually made out the base of antlers and an ear of a buck, the buck he wanted.

The whitetail was only bedded 50 yards away, but there was no way he could get a bullet through the tangle of stems between them. He would have to wait for the buck to stand up and step in the open. When the two bucks Jack saw earlier returned at 10:40 a.m., he got the opportunity he was waiting for. As the mature whitetail scoring 155 4/8 got up to chase the smaller bucks off, Eddy took his shot. That buck was 5 1/2 years old and had a live weight of 235 pounds.

If it weren't for Jack's increasing difficulty getting around, he might have bagged a state record typical during the fall of 1996. His scouting during 1996 put him onto a buck that he knew had a Boone and Crockett qualifying rack (minimum of 170). He said the antlers didn't have much of a spread, but the tines were long, as long as 14 inches. Unfortunately, Jack had surgery and was not able to hunt during the '96 season.

However, he told a close friend about the booner and convinced him to try for the

Expert Senior Citizen

Jack with the 13-pint nontypical netting 162 6/8 that he got in Gratiot County on opening day of the 1995 season. Photo courtesy Jack Van Riper.

deer. The guy managed to bag the buck on the second day of the season, but by then one of the beams had been shot off beyond the second tine. Based on the measurements of the antler that remained and what the dimensions of the missing antler should have been, Jack and his friend figured the rack would have scored 204.

Jack has not let the fact that he has used a walker to get around since 1997 impair his hunting for trophy bucks. He took a pair of book bucks each year from 1998 through 2000. He collected a pair of 10-pointers with his .270 at the age of 74 from Saginaw County during 1998 that scored 138 and 150 6/8.

During the 1999 season, he got a 12-pointer in Saginaw County that scored 162 and a 10-point from Gratiot County that measured 154 4/8. He scored on one buck from each county during 2000, too. A Saginaw County 11-point that measured 144 fell to his rifle on opening day and a 9-point that measured 137 5/8 was tagged in Gratiot County on November 20.

There's an interesting story behind the 11-pointer Eddy shot in Saginaw County on November 15, 2000. He said that whitetail was laid up on 200 acres of land nobody has permission to hunt that adjoins property he hunts. Even though the refuge is off limits to hunting, Jack said trespassers (poachers) invariably try to sneak on the property on the first day of firearms season every year.

He used that knowledge to his advantage. When a trespasser entered the land that was supposed to be off limits on the 15th, he immediately jumped the buck Jack had been watching and pushed it right into him. Intimate knowledge of the habits of the bucks he hunts as well as hunting pressure, has made Eddy the most successful senior citizen hunter in the state.

His entries have dominated the senior division of the Michigan records since 1992. He has taken five first places in that category and four seconds during nine years of hunting. During 1999, he took first place for both typical and nontypical entries in the senior division. The year before, he took first and second place in the typical category. The 11-pointer scoring 144 that Jack bagged during 2000 came in second place in the senior division, with the 9-point measuring 137 5/8, taking third.

One of Eddy's secrets to success on big bucks over the years is using all of the critters in the woods to his advantage, like those chickadees that tipped him off to the presence of the bedded buck he shot during 1997. He said that was the third book buck that chickadees had tipped him off to.

"If you learn to use the creatures in the woods like red squirrels, crows and chickadees, you will see more game," Jack said. "I always carry a crow call to signal hunting partners without making the alarm call. The relaxed calls of a crow will calm deer. The alarm call will have the opposite effect. Deer use crows and other animals as sentinels."

Scouting is also of paramount importance. Jack scouts seven to eight months out of the year. He uses 8 power binoculars to do a lot of scouting from a distance, doing so from vantage points that allow him to watch large expanses of open habitat.

Expert Senior Citizen

He said alfalfa fields are where bucks first go when their antlers are developing. Even though racks may only be beginning to show during the spring, he doesn't have any trouble telling the mature bucks from the youngsters. He commented that bucks that are at least five years old will look like a sway back horse. They will also usually have larger bodies than their younger counterparts.

Once Jack gets a line on a mature buck, he learns as much as he can about that deer, following it when ever possible, while, at the same time trying not to disturb the animal. He uses what he learns about a buck to try to determine where to ambush it when the season arrives. The more time you spend in the field, the more you will learn, according to Eddy. It's as simple as that.

The locations that Jack hunts play an important role in his consistent success on big bucks, too. There's good genetics for antler development in the spots he has access to in Gratiot and Saginaw Counties. The 8-pointer Eddy shot in Gratiot County during 1994, for example, which scored 140 6/8, was only 2 1/2 years old.

Another trait that both tracts have in common is that they have the only cover within 3/4-of-a-mile. Beans are one of the major crops grown in those areas. Once the beans are harvested, there's no cover left, except on the parcels where Jack hunts. The biggest bucks are going to go where there's cover.

Eddy does almost all of his deer hunting in southern Michigan on private property and he does everything he can to maintain a good relationship with landowners. He's contacted landowners himself to obtain permission to hunt in many cases, but he's been invited to hunt on some parcels due to his reputation as a knowledgeable deer hunter. He was first invited to hunt the property in Gratiot County where he's taken seven book deer during 1989.

The group of five men who hunted there knew of at least four trophy bucks that inhabited the parcel, but had been unable to get a shot at them. They contacted Eddy for advice toward the end of the '89 firearms season. Jack went with them to the property on November 29. After looking the situation over, he posted the men in likely spots and drives were conducted to move the deer out of the brush.

Three of the four mature bucks were tagged that day and Jack got one of them, a big 8-pointer with 12-inch tines that scored 140 1/8. He said a total of 52 deer were pushed out of the brush during drives that memorable day. He's been invited back to hunt the property every year since then.

Jack has taken a number of book bucks on drives besides that first one from Gratiot County. The first whitetail he shot that qualified for state records, for instance, was taken on a drive conducted by his father during 1942 in Kalkaska County along the banks of the Manistee River. The 10-pointer scoring 137 3/8 was with a pair of does. His father also pushed his Houghton County buck that's in the records, to him during 1966.

Being able to shoot well has been a key ingredient in Eddy's success on big bucks over the years and his advice to others is to, "Learn how to shoot. All the effort that goes into getting a shot at a book buck is for naught if you can't hit 'em."

He said shooting trap is excellent practice for deer hunters who may get shooting at running deer on drives or while stillhunting.

"Shoot at running deer with both eyes open, just like you would during a round of trap," Jack said. "Shoot as the crosshairs pass the spot you want to hit. Swing through the target. That's a deadly way to shoot if your gun fits you."

The experienced big buck hunter said it's also important for hunters to be as scent free as possible by showering before hunting, if possible. He uses Kirk's Hardwater Casteel Soap when showering. He said it's available from most supermarkets.

Another bit of advice from the expert is to eliminate any rattles from your pockets that might give your location away. He takes his keys and change out of his pockets to eliminate that potential source of noise. Extra rifle shells are put singly in pockets or secured elsewhere, so that they can't make any noise either.

Although Jack has taken most of his book bucks from blinds while posted in promising spots or on drives, he scored on at least one while stillhunting in Shiawassee County during 1975. That whitetail was a 3 1/2-year-old 9-point that had a 24-inch spread. Those antlers measured 146 7/8.

"It was the last day of the season and I just got permission to hunt that property the day before," Jack told me. "A guy I was hunting with the previous day missed a big buck and I wanted to find out if the deer was still there. It was 60 degrees with a light rain, a beautiful day to hunt.

"I was pussyfooting into the hunting area when I heard shooting from the road that alerted me to the presence of the buck. When I saw the deer it looked like the Hartford Elk coming toward me. He stopped right at 100 yards. I just had my shotgun scoped and it's a good thing."

Jack said that hunters can sometimes score on bucks by checking out small patches of cover that others ignore because they think the spot is too small to hold deer. He shot a 10 1/2-year-old whitetail from such a hideout in 1977. The buck was so old that his 7-point antlers were going downhill, so they didn't qualify for a spot in state records. The rack was also broken from fighting.

The buck was laid up in a small pothole in a field. The ground was wet there, preventing cultivation. Jack said the pothole was smaller than an average house. He visited the pothole 11 days in a row because he had seen deer using it before. On the 11th day, a buck and doe came out of the pothole when he was within 30 feet of the cover. He made a 40 yard running shot on the whitetail with his shotgun.

Although Jack has had plenty of deer hunting experience, he didn't start hunting whitetails as young as many of today's youngsters. He was 17 when he hunted deer for the first time. He went with friends that year. He said he got lost a lot back then and his father got tired of looking for him.

Eddy deer hunted with his father for the first time when he was 18 near Grayling. He shot a nice 8-pointer on opening day. Jack said he and his father often hunted close together. That way his father could better keep tabs on him, reducing the chances he would get lost.

Another advantage for the young Eddy is that his dad was close by to help him handle the bucks he shot. Invariably, Jack was the one who did the shooting. He said his father never shot a buck in Michigan, although he shot his share in Canada.

Eddy learned the value of passing up young bucks from his father at an early age. His rule was to protect spike bucks during the first week of gun season. Hunters in the party who didn't follow that rule would lose a shirt tail.

Jack said it's essential for hunters who are interested in taking book bucks to pass up the small ones. The young bucks that are let go in southern counties one year will often have antlers large enough to qualify for state records the following year. That's when to take them. Eddy knows from personal experience because he's done it time after time.

What does the 2001 season hold for Jack Eddy? A paragraph in a letter I received from him dated June 26, 2001 contained part of the answer:

"The 2001 season looks promising. At present, I am watching six bucks in three counties that will weigh from 200 to 300 pounds on the hoof. All of these should be 'shooters.' The racks are out past the ears and curving up now."

Jack Eddy displays the impressive antlers of a 10-point he got in Gratiot County on November 15, 1997 that netted 155 4/8. Photo courtesy Jack Van Riper.

Robbie Delliss with the 16-point nontypical he shot in Baraga County during 1989. The antlers netted 198 4/8.

Chapter 15

Baraga County Nontypicals

The Upper Peninsula's Baraga County is one of the best in the state in terms of producing bucks that grow nontypical racks of Boone and Crockett proportions. No less than eight racks of that caliber that score a minimum of 195 are listed in state records compiled by Commemorative Bucks of Michigan (CBM). The bucks that grew those antlers were shot between 1912 and 1989.

Robbie Delliss from Michigamme was the lucky hunter who claimed the most recent B&C nontypical from the county. It's a 16-pointer that measured 198 4/8. He collected the whitetail on November 19, 1989 in a location where he and his hunting partners had taken a number of nice bucks over the years. Two years earlier, for example, Delliss downed a 9-pointer that weighed the same as his booner - 200 pounds dressed - but it had considerably smaller antlers.

The terrain Delliss hunts is rugged and hilly with a capital H. Some people refer to the bigger "hills" as mountains. The habitat is a mix of hardwood trees and swamps. The biggest bucks are often found either on top of the highest ridges or down low in the thickest swamps in this country where they are seldom bothered. Robbie got his booner along the edge of a big swamp.

The B&C 16-point that Delliss shot during '89 showed up at 8:45 a.m. at a spot Robbie had been baiting with apples. He said the buck was actually walking on a skid trail that parallels the edge of the swamp. He took a 50 yard shot with an old .30-30 passed down to him from his grandfather and the buck ran off. Delliss said he only saw the deer's right antler and that beam has a typical structure with five main points. Most of the antler mass and nontypical points are on the left side, so Robbie didn't realize how big of a rack the buck had at the time he shot it.

Inspite of a good hit in a shoulder, Delliss had to trail the trophy whitetail to recover it. Fortunately, there was snow on the ground. Hair was on the snow where Robbie's bullet struck the buck, but there was no blood. He said he followed the whitetail's

117

tracks for a while before blood started appearing along its trail.

Delliss jumped the buck once after following it for 15 to 20 minutes without getting a shot at it, but he managed to finish the buck when he caught up to it a second time. He estimated that he followed the exceptional deer a quarter mile before finally getting it. The whitetail's age was estimated to be 3 1/2. If that age was accurate, the deer exhibited excellent antler development for a U.P. buck.

As luck would have it, Robbie bagged another trophy nontypical whitetail from the same spot during 1990 on November 16 at 4:45 p.m. The rack that buck grew wasn't as large as the one he got the year before, having two fewer points, but the body was bigger. The antlers scored 163 2/8 and the carcass had a dressed weight of 235 pounds.

"When I got that 14-pointer during 1990, the conditions were totally opposite of what they had been the year before," Delliss said. "It was 60 degrees and there was no snow on the ground. It was so warm, I was wearing a tee shirt when I shot that buck. It was a beautiful sunny day.

"The year before, it was 10 below zero and there was two feet of snow on the ground. The buck I shot during '90 was on the same skid trail the 16-pointer was on when I shot him, but he was coming from the east. The bigger buck came from the west. I dropped the smaller nontypical 50 feet from where I shot the booner.

"I had my .30-30 with me again, but this time I aimed for the neck. I buckled him right there. I think that buck was a brother of the deer I shot during 1989. The 16-pointer was 3 1/2 and the 14 I shot a year later was 4 1/2."

The fact that Delliss bagged a pair of trophy nontypicals that might have been brothers from the same spot two years in a row is amazing enough, but what's even more spectacular is Robbie's son Kevin almost shot a buck that was much bigger than the 14-pointer the day before, which was opening day of the 1990 firearms season.

"My boy was with me when I shot the 14-point," Delliss said. "The day before, he missed a bigger buck at 11:00 a.m. He got to looking at all of the points on the antlers and he got buck fever. The buck he missed had an enormous rack.

"I had my .30-30 and could have backed him up, but he had been shooting so good, I didn't think I needed to. When I saw the 14-point the next day, I handed the rifle to the boy and he handed it back. He was too nervous."

And the 14-point nontypical was not the last big buck Robbie shot from his hot spot.

"I gave the spot a break for a while," Delliss said. "Then a couple of years later, I took a 12-point out of there. And then a 10 and an 8 and a couple more 10s. I never had the others measured, so I don't know what they scored. A buck is a buck."

That's true enough, but each set of antlers is different and measurements vary accordingly. However, I can understand why Robbie might not be interested in measuring racks that are smaller than the two whoppers he already has hanging on his wall.

Delliss said you never know when you are going to see a big buck in the country he hunts, that's why he hunts from dark to dark. However, he added that it's common to see trophy whitetails during the middle of day. That is when his son missed what could have been his first trophy whitetail.

Former Ishpeming resident Dennis Bess had bagged the most recent B&C nontypical from Baraga County until 1989. He got a 15-pointer on November 20, 1981 that measured 202 6/8. Bess said he selected a stand overlooking a spot where he hoped to see a big buck. A couple of large antler rubbed trees in the vicinity were the clues that tipped him off to the whitetail's presence.

He hunted the location with a view of a swamp edge every day starting November 15. It was the sixth day of the season before he saw the buck and the animal appeared

Delliss with the smaller nontypical he shot from the same spot during 1990 that he thinks might be a brother to the booner. Robbie's son missed a bigger buck the day before while sitting with his father.

Dennis Bess with the 15-point nontypical he shot on November 20, 1981 that measured 202 6/8.

when he least expected to see it. Minutes before the bruiser made its appearance, a pair of other hunters were talking on a logging road immediately behind Bess. He figured the noise they made would be enough to spook any whitetails within ear shot.

Apparently the booner didn't hear their voices. Bess watched the other hunters fade away and turned back facing the swamp in time to see the buck walk into view at 8:20 a.m. Dennis said he knew the deer was a shooter even though he only saw a portion of its rack.

Most of the antlers were obscured from view when Bess shot the whitetail. He was in for a shock as it took off running and he got a much better view of its headgear. Dennis fired two more rounds from his rifle at the deer, both of which connected, before the buck dropped.

Bess was even more impressed with the size of the antlers when he reached the fallen whitetail than he had been after his first shot. It takes a lot of antler to reach 200 inches much less exceed that number. The antlers weren't the only thing big about the deer. It's body was also bigger than most, dressing out at 243 pounds.

Dennis was hunting out of a camp in Baraga County with seven family members when he got his booner and he wasn't the only one to score that fall. In fact, all but one member of the party managed to bag bucks. Two of the six remaining whitetails tagged by the Bess family had 9-point racks, one had 8 and the remaining whitetails had 3, 4 and 5-point antlers.

The reason the eighth member of the group didn't fill his tag is not because he didn't have an opportunity to. He missed a big buck that was thought to have at least a 10-point rack.

Robert Heikkinen from L'anse bagged Baraga County's next most recent B&C nontypical on November 15, 1976. It's a 14-pointer scoring 199.

The weather was unseasonably cold that year. After hunting until noon without filling a tag, Heikkinen offered to go back to camp to prepare dinner so his father and friend Irving Santti could continue hunting. It was a thoughtful gesture that put him in position to bag a world class buck. As Heikkinen drove toward camp, a pair of bucks ran across the road near the Skanee Airport, interrupting Robert's plans.

An 8-point was in the lead, followed by the much bigger animal. There was snow on the ground, so Robert picked up the buck's tracks where they went in the woods and followed them. He jumped them several times, but wasn't able to get a shot. He finally came to a knoll, with the tracks going around the right side of it.

"I had a feeling that those bucks were on the back side of that hill," Robert wrote. "So instead of following the tracks, I decided to sneak up the hill. When I reached the top, I peered over and there he was laying behind a brushpile with his massive rack blending in with the brush. I took a deep breath and squeezed the trigger. The Hardford of Skanee dropped his head and never ran again."

Baraga County's highest scoring nontypical was shot by Richard Washington from Cheboygan when he was 19 years old on opening day of the 1937 season. Washington said the book buck simply walked out 50 yards away into a cleared survey line he was watching and he shot it with a .30-30. The 29-pointer scored 214.

Harry Stamman of Genesee took the county's second highest scoring nontypical during the 1953 season. The 16-point whitetail measured 205. Two of its 16-points are drop tines.

Stamman was hunting from a stand that was a 1 1/4-mile walk from where he parked his vehicle when he got the trophy deer. The buck was trotting at a distance of 100 to 125 yards at 9:00 a.m. when Stamman shot it with a 7 mm Mauser. His bullet struck the deer in the heart. The deer was aged at 4 1/2 and weighed 220 pounds after hanging for a week.

The late John Dougherty shot the first nontypical booner that's listed in state records. He got it in 1912. It's a 19-point that scored 197 4/8.

Dougherty was 31 years old when he got the whitetail, according to his daughter, who now owns the head. She said that the annual bag limit was six deer the year he got the exceptional buck. It took two shots from her father's .30-30 to bring the buck down along a railroad grade. The deer was estimated to weigh 300 pounds.

Robert Heikkinen from L'anse with 14-point nontypical he bagged on November 15, 1976 after tracking it in the snow. Photo courtesy Robert Heikkinen.

Richard Washington with Baraga County's highest scoring nontypical. The 19-pointer scored 214. Washington shot the buck in 1937 when he was 19 years old.

Author

Richard P. Smith from Marquette, Michigan is only the second person in Michigan to collect a CBM Grand Slam. To complete such a feat, a hunter must shoot deer, bear, elk and turkey that qualify for listing in state records maintained by Commemorative Bucks of Michigan (CBM). It took Smith a liftetime of hunting in the state to achieve the goal. His slam was completed on November 3, 2000 when he bagged a turkey that qualified for CBM records.

The author of this book has been writing about the biggest bucks bagged by hunters in his home state since the early 1980s. What he has learned about whitetail hunting by interviewing those hunters has made him a better hunter. He bagged a trophy 10-pointer during November of 1999 in Saskatchewan that grossed 166 5/8 and netted 163 7/8, qualifying for honorable mention in Boone and Crockett Records. His best Michigan buck is an 11-pointer that netted 148 4/8.

Smith is an award winning outdoor writer and photographer who has been hunting whitetail deer and black bear for almost 40 years. The author/photographer is a recognized expert on whitetail deer and black bear behavior and biology as well as hunting these popular big game animals. One of his honors was receipt of the coveted Ben East Prize for 1997 from the Michigan United Conservation Clubs for conservation journalism about bear management. He also received the Outdoor Journalist of the Year Award from the Flint, Michigan Chapter of Safari Club International the same year.

The author is a nationally recognized writer, photographer and speaker who has written 18 books and more than a thousand magazine articles, specializing in all types of wildlife, but especially whitetails and black bear. He writes a Regional Report about happenings in the Upper Peninsula of Michigan for Michigan Out-of-Doors Magazine and contributes regularly to Michigan Sportsman, Michigan Hunting & Fishing, Woods-N-Water News and Upper Michigan Outdoor Journal. His writing and photography appear regularly in national magazines including Deer & Deer Hunting, Whitetail Strategies, North American Whitetail, American Hunter, North American Hunter, Outdoor Life, Bowhunter and Harris Publications.

Author Richard P. Smith with his best typical whitetail, a 10-point scoring 163 7/8. What he has learned by interviewing hunters who have taken Michigan's biggest bucks has made him a better deer hunter.

Books by Richard P. Smith

Great Michigan Deer Tales, Book 1- Learn How, Where and When some of the state's Biggest Bucks were bagged, including a Boone & Crockett bow kill taken by Mitch Rompola from Traverse City. Read about whitetails with the largest ANTLERS as well as those that were the HEAVIEST and OLDEST. If you are interested in bagging a BOOK BUCK in Michigan, studying this collection of success stories will help make it happen. There's no better way to learn than from those who have already accomplished the feat. (128 pages; 40 photos)
Price: $15.50 postpaid

Great Michigan Deer Tales, Book 2 - More Great Deer Tales from Michigan. Read about the highest scoring typical ever recorded for Michigan through 1997 seasons. Find out about the biggest bucks bagged by **women** in the state. Learn about trophy bucks with **locked antlers**. Read about a trophy rack recovered after almost 40 years and the end of a 70-year mystery surrounding a B&C nontypical. If you haven't gotten the first book yet, you will want to get both. (128 pages; 46 photos)
Price: $16.50 postpaid; Set of Book 1 & 2 - $28 (save $4)

Great Michigan Deer Tales, Book 3 - This book contains what might be the state's best deer tale ever about North America's best buck ever taken by a one-of-a-kind whitetail hunter. Two chapters are devoted to unraveling the mystery behind a whopper 12-pointer scoring more than the current world record that Mitch Rompola shot with bow and arrow during 1998. Other chapters are devoted to a hunt shared by a father and son on which the year's biggest buck was bagged, a 14-year-old whose first deer was a booner, a woman who bagged a state record whitetail with the help of her husband, a bowhunter who collected a world class buck on his first day of hunting, one of the state's most successful senior citizens and much, much more.
Price: $16.50 postpaid; Set of Book 1, 2 & 3- $40 (save $8.50)

Stand Hunting for Whitetails - Learn the best places to hunt, most productive times, dressing for -20 F, how to hunt safely above the ground and how to avoid being detected by deer from ground and elevated stands. Read about Boone and Crockett bucks and a hunt with baseball great **Wade Boggs**. Stand hunting is the most popular and effective whitetail hunting method. **Learn how to do it more effectively!**
 (256 pages; 181 photos)
Price: $18.50 postpaid

Tracking Wounded Deer - 2nd Edition - Learn how to recover all of the deer you shoot by reading blood sign, tracking after dark and in the snow and using a string tracker. Decide when to begin tracking, determine type of hit and distinguish between tracks of wounded and healthy deer. This book is must reading for bowhunters since trailing arrowed deer is part of every successful hunt. Eight pages of color photos show blood and hair sign. (160 pages; 72 photos)
Price: $19.50 postpaid

Deer Hunting - 2nd Edition - This best selling book was so popular it was updated to include even more information and photographs. Learn all you need to know to successfully hunt whitetails and mule deer. There are bonus chapters on deer biology and management, hunting ethics and more. For beginners or experienced veterans like the author. (260 pages; 139 photos)
Price: $18.00 postpaid

MICHIGAN BIG GAME RECORDS (1ST-3RD EDITIONS) - The 3rd edition is a bigger and better reference for Michigan hunters with the addition of turkey records. This 272-page volume continues the tradition of providing the best and latest information about trophy deer, bear and elk hunting in the state. The who, how, where and when of trophy kills from 1989-1992 are covered in the 3rd edition. Those taken from 1986-'88 are discussed in the 256-page 2nd edition and trophies taken through 1985 are covered in the 1st edition (216 pages). Each edition of the record book has different chapters about big game hunting in Michigan, with emphasis on deer, and hundreds of photos. You will want to own a set of all three books to become one of the state's most knowledgeable big game hunters. **We are sold out of the 4th edition.**
All three editions remaining are offered in both hard(HC) and soft(SC) cover versions.
**Price: Set of 3(SC) $55, 2nd &3rd Editions(SC) $21 each, 1st Edition $18
Set of 3(HC) $113, 1st,2nd,& 3rd Editions(HC) $39 each**

Animal Tracks & Signs Of North America - It's the first guide book including actual photos of wildlife tracks and sign rather than sketches. Bonus chapters cover aging tracks, tracking wildlife and much more. (271 pages; 200 photos)
Price: $20 postpaid.

Understanding Michigan Black Bear - 2nd Edition- Learn all about Michigan black bears; their habits, life history and behavior in addition to how to avoid problems from them when in bear country. One of the chapters is a history of bear attacks. The text also provides valuable insights into bear research and management in the state. (256 pages; 126 photos)
Price: $19.50 postpaid

Book Order Form

Quantity   **Price**

_____ Great Michigan Deer Tales, Book 1 ($15.50) _____

_____ Great Michigan Deer Tales, Book 2 ($16.50); _____
_____   Set of Book 1 & 2 - ($28) _____

_____ Great Michigan Deer Tales, Book 3 ($16.50); _____
_____   Set of Book 1, 2 & 3 - ($40) _____

_____ Stand Hunting for Whitetails ($18.50) _____

_____ Tracking Wounded Deer - 2nd Edition ($19.50) _____

_____ Deer Hunting - 2nd Edition ($18.00) _____

_____ Michigan Big Game Records (Specify edition) _____

_____ Animal Tracks & Signs Of North America ($20) _____

_____ Understanding Michigan Black Bear - 2nd Edition ($19.50) _____

                                                        Total Payment Enclosed _____

Prices include postage and handling. Make checks payable to:

Smith Publications

Please send U.S. funds.
Canadian orders add $1/book(Parcel Post) or $3/book(Air Mail).

Name _____

Address _____

City _____ State/Zip _____

Phone# _____
        (Phone # needed for credit card orders)

Circle card type:
MC/Visa # _____

Expiration Date _____ Signature _____

Send orders to: Smith Publications
                        814 Clark St.
                        Marquette, MI 49855

                            www.exploringthenorth.com/smith/smith.html/